90-pound heavyweight 'the Life and Triumph of Janet Barnes', Celebrate the legacy of her unsinkable and unstoppable fighting spirit!
© May 10, 2015 (Mother's Day) Angela Barnes ISBN: 978-1-938121-05-0
Library of Congress 2015903763

This book you are now reading, includes the complete original book titled 90-pound heavyweight Janet Barnes, 'Her Story, Words and Life in Vignette'. (Mother's birthday book)
© 2011 Angela Barnes ISBN 978-1-938121-02-9

Published, Distributed and Printed in the USA
Heart Spoken Words LLC
331 Chamberlin Avenue, Fairview Heights IL 62208
618-398-4357
www.heartspokenwords.com
publisher@heartspokenwords.com

This material has been written and published solely for sharing the life of Janet Barnes, and is presented as reliably and honestly as possible.

The information presented in this book represents the view of the author as of the date of publication. This view is based upon research and personal experience.

The author expressly reserves the right to alter and update her opinion in the future if conditions so warrant.

90-POUND HEAVYWEIGHT
the Life and Triumph of Janet Barnes

Once upon a time there were four people named
EVERYBODY, SOMEBODY, ANYBODY and NOBODY.
When there was an important job to be done, EVERYBODY
was sure that SOMEBODY would do it.
ANYBODY could have done it, but NOBODY did.
When NOBODY did it, SOMEBODY got angry because it was
EVERYBODY'S job.
EVERYBODY thought that ANYBODY would do it, but
NOBODY realized that EVERYBODY wouldn't do it.
So it ended up that EVERYBODY blamed SOMEBODY when
NOBODY did what ANYBODY could have done in the first
place.

Author Unknown

MOTHER DID SOMETHING
AND THEN SHE DID MORE!

Contents

Forward: Reverend Annie P. Clark 6

Introduction: Dear Reader 8

Prologue: My Life by Janet Barnes 9

Wabi---Sabi Mother 16

Book One: '90 pound heavyweight Janet Barnes' 18

    Her Story, Words and Life in Vignette

She's Not Confined 24

May You Experience 31

    Section One: Life Before Daddy 32

    Section Two: Life With Daddy 43

        Wedding Vow 47

    Section Three: Life After Daddy 59

My Life in Haiku by Janet Barnes 93

Personal Information 97

Do It Again, Grandma! 99

Epilogue 100

Book Two: MORE: Mother's Letters, Writings, Thoughts ... 101

10 Rules for a Happy Marriage 116

I Am the Most Fortunate of People 117

MORE: Comments, Tributes, Prayers 132

The Human Factor 142

A Few Medical Updates 147

Mother's Unforgettable Words 154

Angela's Voice 155

What Do I Know? 157

Happy Mother's Day 159

24 and 48 Hours 166

Allegory fo the Long Spoons 167

Legacy Foundation 169

Post Script 171

Yes Mother, You Did Enough! 172

About the Author 173

Acknowledgements

A heartfelt thank you from me and mother, goes out to so many special people, known and unknown directly to us, who made this new book possible.

Thanks to Reverend Annie P. Clark for her support, both tangibly and emotionally and the wonderful foreword she offered for this book.

To Vaneese Shaw for the photo help she continued to provide so that you are seeing the best I can offer you and for her caring and friendship to me, my husband and this goal of sharing mother.

To my amazing husband, Bob (Robert Haug) who put up with the time it took---the real time working, the time trying, crying and coming to peace with me growing tall enough to do the task of sharing without taint or blame. I think I achieved that.

I also acknowledge and thank you who knew mother during her life, and those that met her via Facebook, the website, the sharing by others, or by me maybe just meeting and talking to you after the accident. Your involvement, sincere prayers, comments and support encouraged me and helped mother beyond words...

...I am grateful for you today, who are taking time to learn of her strength and fearless life, and for getting to know the miracle and gift she was and continues to share with all of us.

Thank You!

Foreword

"Differently abled" is how Janet Barnes described herself. Here is a woman who fully understood that she had abilities and capabilities that went far above and beyond what her physical stature implied. Janet knew that there was something within her that enabled her to call forth the strength and courage to live fully as a wise and productive being. She utilized skills that so many "other abled" persons fail to recognize.

This courageous woman knew that she could and would overcome what others thought of as a handicap. She continuously pursued the richness of her unlimited spiritual and mental gifts. Not only was she gainfully employed, but was one of the early "work at home" pioneers.

Read how this 90-pound wonder of a woman drank from "the waters of life." Read how she inspired (and continues to inspire) others through her unstoppable desire to live independently, to continuously learn, and to always share what she learned. Read her beautiful poems and enjoy her artwork. After reading about her, I had the joy of meeting Janet Barnes in person. Although she could hardly speak above a whisper, her warm smile and bright eyes allowed me to see past her physical condition. I am so thankful for the privilege of spending a few moments of time with this remarkable woman who always said, "Yes!" to life.

Angela Barnes shares her mother with us. Through writing about her mother, Angela regains her "voice" – which had been silent. Let her words and memories inspire each of us to visit our innate abilities. Let this poignant story of how a daughter lived with a "differently abled" mother, teach what strength there is at the very depths of our being. Let Angela reveal what is important – determination, faith in one's self, and unconditional love. Let the life of Janet Barnes, as told by her daughter Angela, be a catalyst for all of us to be all that we are meant to be.

Again, let the words, actions and faith of Janet reveal to each of us how we, too, can rise above any and all of our self-imposed limitations. Let her determination be a guide for us to live a life filled with potential, peace, purpose and joy.

My life certainly is richer because I met Janet Barnes, a 90-pound heavy-weight wonder of a woman.

Reverend Annie P. Clark

Introduction

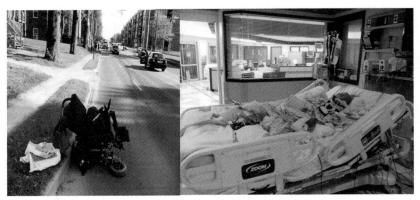

Dear Reader,

My mother, Janet Barnes, at the age of 83 was in a serious accident on April 23, 2012. She was hit by a car wheeling home (in her wheelchair). Once again, she proved and lived her unsinkable spirit--her belief that life is the most precious gift of all! Most of her bones were broken. The fear, challenge, and fight to survive continued and demonstrated her strong and faith filled outlook on life. This book is about her life and triumph--in her own words. It is a good representation of a remarkable, independent, less than '90-pound heavyweight' who, until her last fighting breath, September 9, 2013, one month before her 85th birthday, lived, thrived, championed and loved life!

Book One, '90-pound heavyweight, Janet Barnes, Her Story, Words and Life in Vignette', was written and completed for her 83rd birthday, with her complete involvement verifying the words and stories.

The accident was one month after her confirmation into Guinness World Records--a feat she deemed fair. I'm just happy it was completed. I've made minimal edits to the original birthday book included here.

In Book Two, you have new sharing by mother entitled MORE. Much of this 'new' was seemingly miraculously discovered after her death. I also share my journey with her, and the comments and impressions of the many lives she touched and changed, including the medical industry, and the paradigm shifts experienced by so many.

Prologue: My Life by Janet Barnes

I am a living, breathing person. According to some of the religious programs I watch, this breathing is an important factor. We breathe in all that we breathe in--we grow. To grow, I feel we must remember. I was not given the gift of spelling. Have a little more than normal mathematical ability. I was given or have developed a determined inhibited ego--a really super strong super ego, and a special ability to remember. Who could ask for more?

I think, I feel, and I remember. When you remember the result of each experience, you can learn from it, thereby preventing some mistakes. I'm most fortunate in having the ability to learn from the mistakes of others. I've been talented in finding books to substantiate what I think or feel. Then I am secure enough to speak about it.

One of my most authentic books said we pick our parents so we can accomplish whatever we are wanting to accomplish in this life. I told one of my doctors once, "If I knew I wasn't going to be able to get out of bed, I didn't use good judgment in picking my parents." It's been different and difficult, but so far, never impossible. I couldn't have had better training for my role as a physically challenged child and adult.

I'm sure I'm as appreciative and grateful as anyone for everything. I'm totally pleased with the life I've lived, and am living.

My parents were young, immature adults. I was their first child. They knew nothing about taking care of a child, and they never learned much about taking care of one like me. I couldn't sit alone. My first grade teacher taught me to walk on crutches when I was six. I was left in bed or sometimes propped up with a pillow on a couch. I had more than enough time alone, just thinking, to develop exhilarating thought processes. Also, mind over matter experience developed the ability to wait hours between bathroom trips. I never cried or fussed. My inhibited ego didn't permit it. I just waited.

It's true--the person who yells the loudest, like the wheel that squeaks the loudest, gets more attention than the one which is quiet. My folks caused my inhibited ego. If I waited and didn't disturb them until they were ready to come to me, they were more pleasant. I'm sure being inhibited has contributed in my accomplishments. I have developed more patience than should be allowed. This is good in the over-all picture. **I added the determination.**

I realized about nine years ago I had been neglected. There were no rulings on child neglect then. I was resentful for a while, and I really believed if you have reason for resentment and aren't, you are stupid. By permitting myself to feel this, without guilt, these feelings of resentment are gone.

My parents cared for me to the best of their ability. No one can do more. They overdid this, not spoiling me a bit. I had a cousin 18 months older than me born with a dislocated hip. She was spoiled until she was a monster. My people worked overtime at not spoiling me. I was taught really good to accept and not fuss. To explain what I mean by neglect, my baby brother and I were left alone at night while our parents went out to taverns to drink. These memories are from the age frame of, Donny--one or two, me--three or four.

During prohibition the parties were at our house, and we weren't left alone, except once. Pretty sure I was almost three when some man drugged my mother and ran off with her. My dad went after them. It was a long time before they came home. This kind of stuff was scary. Donny would scream during the daytime -- he did sleep at night.

It was when they started going to taverns that life for me was no fun. I would lay awake until they came home, because there was less fear waiting for them to get up in the morning if I knew they were home. This getting up is where they trained me to be a pleasant, appreciative, physically dependent person. When they would finally get up, after coffee and fussing about who was going to *have to* get me up--that's the expression they used (who was going to *have to* get me up.) That bothered me. I don't know why they fussed, it was always mother. If I didn't greet her with a smiling face she went away and came back later. This developed good kidney and bladder control, and you learn quickly to be pleasant. I'm not displeased with my training. I've been hurt, but I'm not bitter.

I can't stand waste. To have a hurt that was not compensated for with knowledge and understanding, would be a hurt for no purpose. It would be wasted. I will find good in everything. I am physically dependent, and I should be pleasant and have appreciation. I am--I do. I would be pleasant and appreciative, even if I shouldn't be, from being bothered by the expression "who was going to *have to* get me up."

I learned to appreciate responsibility, to accept it as if it were a God-given privilege. I'm not sure if we accept responsibility in proportion to our ability to provide, or if our ability to provide depends on how much responsibility we gather for ourselves. Somehow it did balance.

All I knew for sure about the young man I married (Harold) was that he loved me. I was 21 years old when we met. He wheeled to me each morning for 18 months, climbed 14 steps, pulling his manual chair after him, to get to me to put my shoes and socks on and help me to a sitting position. I could walk to the bathroom and finish dressing. No one had ever been that dependable. He didn't fuss.

This was love. We didn't know if I could be a wife or mother, if he could be a husband or dad. Didn't know if he could ever get a job. There was no help for people in wheelchairs then. He had only a 4th grade tangible education. That's all the schooling the hospital (Missouri Baptist Hospital) provided for him. Prospects for a job were not good. He had just quit his job at Missouri Baptist hospital where he had been raised as an orphan from 5 to 15. At 15 the doctor who was sponsoring him was killed. The hospital let Harold work for his keep, and I guess some spending money. He worked there until he was 22. I didn't know any details of why he quit until five years later. I didn't judge. I wondered. I wouldn't have quit a job until I had one to go to. So you won't judge, I'll tell you quickly why he quit. His uncle Howard came to a birthday party. The uncle had been a member of the board at the hospital. He said Harold had asked for a $5 dollar a month raise after working there for seven years. When they refused, he quit. Uncle Howard added, "they had to hire five people at full pay to do the work Harold was doing."

I had finished high school and a course in photo retouching. I didn't have much of a job. I worked at home--piece work. I had a roof over my head and food to eat. Harold was staying with his brother on the 3rd floor. He had to leave his wheelchair on the sidewalk. Once it was stolen. Housing and food doesn't cost any more for two than one. Two really can live as cheap as one. He bought a city license permitting him to sell wherever there were people. We paid a percentage to work picnics--he sold costume jewelry, balloons, and carnival supplies. We also worked Shrine conventions on consignment for a percentage. We sold Moolah Temple jewelry and license plate holders. We continued to work these Shrine conventions on weekends after Harold had steady work. I didn't do any selling. I packed lunches, took care of the kids, and talked to Harold on the trips home to keep him from falling asleep. We had a ham radio. He worked as cashier at a car wash--later at Dynacraft Metal Finishing Company. This place had government contracts. There were layoffs. Finally he got a permanent job at Alexian Brothers Hospital taking care of their switchboard. His title: PBX Operator. He had filled in for the operator at Missouri Baptist Hospital from nine years old on.

We did fine. Whatever Harold could make, I could make it be enough. I always worked and made a little. Enough for a few extras. Even if I could have, I wouldn't have made more than Harold. I wanted him to know for sure he was the provider. We were always able to give the kids all that they needed, and some of what they wanted.

Being physically challenged wasn't a problem--didn't interfere with us living a normal life. We worked harder than walking people. Our first apartment was in the building I had lived in when he was helping me up each morning. It had the14 steps. I could get up and down them, but they always scared me.

Harold would get out of his chair, climb the steps on his feet and one hand, and pull his chair up after him. After Angela was born, I didn't get to go out as much as before. We couldn't carry her in or out. Transportation was a Salsbury motor scooter with a side-car. Harold had a rack welded to the back of the sidecar to carry his chair. I put my crutches beside me. We used this until Angela got old enough to want to go bye-bye. After she was walking, we could get her in and out some, and she would have to fit in front of me in the bottom of the side-car. She was terrified of the motor scooter.

We had established credit at Biederman's Furniture Store just before our daughter, Angela, was born. We paid cash for her bed but went in debt for a wardrobe to match it. Each item cost $30.

When Angela was 15 months old, we had arranged for Harold's brother to take us to see the Christmas lights downtown St. Louis. We had her dressed in black patent leather shoes, white anklets, light blue flared skirt with suspenders, a little white blouse with lace. He didn't come for us. Angela cried. The next day we went in $600 debt, bought a '41 Oldsmobile club coupe. Oldsmobile was the only car then that had an automatic transmission. Harold improvised his own hand controls. Now we could take Angela bye-bye.

By the time our second little girl was born (12 noon in the middle of my 23rd birthday), we had outgrown our efficiency apartment. We found a $4,000 house in need of repairs where we could make a porch and ramp to the back door. We did this. The lot was so narrow we had to rent the lot next door to get the car to the back door. We roofed, put new siding on, wall-papered, painted, put in a second bathroom, and paid for it, and outgrew it when Brian, our second boy was born. We traded this little frame house in on a big brick two-family building and started the repair process all over again.

It was at the beginning of my 4th pregnancy that I had what was called a mental breakdown. The psychiatrist, Dr. Lawrence, called me schizophrenic. In reality it was a hormone imbalance. This was established by a psychiatrist at Barnes Hospital years later. Dr. Lawrence gave me eight shock treatments between Brian's 4th and 7th week of conception and kept me on two 25-mg of Thorazine (tablets) every four hours from the 4th week until 5-1/2 months. No way to do a baby. He was born prematurely; both lungs collapsed. He didn't breathe for four days. Has had a learning problem, lot of trouble. He is a special person--a miracle baby. We almost lost him.

I don't think anyone has done any more than Harold and I did, or had any more fun doing it. Harold could do anything but walk, and he did. He wired houses, put in bathrooms and even put a small swimming pool in the back yard. There was never a dull minute. We had enough problems to develop totally active minds. There wasn't anything to quarrel about. We wouldn't have had time to quarrel if there was. We positively came up with our own heaven on earth.

There was a group of sisters, "Sisters of Charity" that would visit us occasionally when the kids were growing up. Sister Mary Lawrence said of us, ours was *a home where love ruled supreme.*

Heart attacks and chest pains were about all we could handle. Harold had to stop working at the hospital. I worked for another year. Harold lived with chest pains for five years. He needed a double bypass, but that wasn't being done readily then, and not being a walking person, recovery was not favorable.

Pain didn't stop him. We had already started raising Chihuahuas and Bassets the year before his heart attack. We enjoyed the dogs and puppies. It was like having babies and kids in the house again. It was great. It increased our income, too. Being personally cared for, and not being left alone, they were so smart. I could write a book about all of these beautiful puppies and dogs. I really should sometime. Dogs think. They remember, and probably are man's best friend.

Harold could deliver them, even turn basset puppies, if needed, most of the time. Couldn't turn Chihuahuas though--there wasn't room. They had to be rushed to the vet for a C-section. We ordered from a veterinary supply catalog. He gave the shots. He could even hit the vein in a Chihuahua if one fainted from low blood sugar and needed glucose. Harold had studied medicine with the interns when he lived at Missouri Baptist Hospital. He took nursing training twice for the knowledge. He didn't get any certificate or acknowledgment. He wasn't expecting any reward for his efforts. Really, he would do anything for anyone at any time--not for merit or reward, but in appreciation of having the ability to do it. I try to be just like him, but I fall a little short. Tonight is writing class night. Must bring this to a close. I think you all can see why I'm still alone after 16 years. You can't settle for less than what you had. There isn't anyone to equal him. I wrote a short story in high school, "It's better to have loved and lost than not to have loved at all." After Harold died, I wasn't sure. You never miss what you haven't had. I'm still not positive the missing is compensated for by the having had, but I think so.

Wabi-Sabi Mother

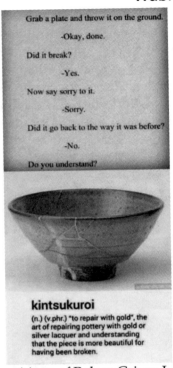

Grab a plate and throw it on the ground.

-Okay, done.

Did it break?

-Yes.

Now say sorry to it.

-Sorry.

Did it go back to the way it was before?

-No.

Do you understand?

kintsukuroi

(n.) (v.phr.) "to repair with gold", the art of repairing pottery with gold or silver lacquer and understanding that the piece is more beautiful for having been broken.

Wabi-Sabi

Is a beauty of things imperfect, impermanent, and incomplete

It is beauty of things modest and humble

It is a beauty of things unconventional

Wabi-Sabi for Artists, Designers, Poets and Philosophers, by Leonard Koren

I was introduced to Wabi-Sabi and its meaning last summer (July 2014) during a retreat I attended at King's House in Belleville, IL. The program, Artist and Spirituality, was remarkably presented by Father Mark Dean who thoroughly researched and generously shared the meaning, origin and current understanding of Wabi-Sabi. I also learned about the thoughts and writings of Robyn Griggs Lawrence who introduced Americans to the 15th century Japanese philosophy of simplicity, serenity and authenticity. Her tender and clear presentation made it real for me.

Revisiting the Wabi Sabi House by Robyn Griggs Lawrence

I found my interpretation of it and I want, no I need--to say what it meant to me when I discovered this word. It was a new idea, and it touched me so deeply that I immediately knew that my mother, Janet Barnes (aka 90-pound heavyweight and Grandma Janet), was the embodiment of Wabi-Sabi. She is Wabi-Sabi Mother! On the outside there were appearances of things that didn't always look whole, healthy or beautiful, but she was.

Hearing the word Wabi-Sabi opened my mind to never-ending possibility--to the concept, the idea and recognition that we are all imperfect in some way. The beautiful actor has a hidden scar. The universe yearns to be sustained, energy fights for distribution, wars demand and damages follow...

I took away the example of a prized vase or delicate belonging that became broken. Instead of discarding it or relegating it to the junk pile, the fractured item was lovingly repaired using an ancient skill known as Kintsukuroi--perhaps with gold paint, and positioned in a place of honor and illuminated where the once injured part is now revered and is a new art extending joy to all that see it. That's mother! Mother's grace under enormous physical challenges and exhausting demands on her tiny body showed this poise, even after the terrible accident that cost so much; did so much damage, including the physical scars to her face and body. All that showed was light and life. At the end she grew more beautiful on the outside, like the light was already shining on her before she died.

Her cheek that was so severely damaged when she was flung from her chair when the car struck her on the street, was repaired and patched with breast tissue, leaving a very noticeable scar. It morphed into more of this beauty, proving again, that nothing that tries to hurt us or break us or scar us is stronger than we are.

My invitation is that you, whoever may be learning this for the first time, and those of you who already know it and may even embrace it, might recognize that Wabi-Sabi is more than one conscious manner of understanding. It is more than mind--more than heart. It is the integration of all thoughts, with recognition that there is an inherent gift inside each and everyone, regardless of the appearance.

Nothing is in a vacuum, and neither am I. Today I see beauty in the uncharted places of my mind where once I, too, gazed on injury, inhumanity or prejudice--not so much anymore. I find my soul is stretching for me to accept this model. This mindset is part of how I get there. I'm grateful. I'm hopeful, and sometimes I remember.

Heart sense (an open heart) permits us to know more than we think we know. It may help us to relate to more than a one or two dimensional view--to more than a broken vase, more than a worn and battered something. Wabi-Sabi Mother--more. That's what I encourage you to carry with you in your heart as you learn more of mother, more of her life, her story, her challenges, her strength and her triumph. I did.

"I've always said, and I mean it. I take what I get
and make the best of it."

Book One:

90-pound heavyweight
JANET BARNES

Her Story, Words and Life
in Vignette

by Angela Barnes

I've made very little edits in this book since I decided not to print the planned second tribute book about mother. Instead, I decided to revise and include both books in one.

I removed the original documentation included for Guinness World Records (GWR), since she was confirmed March 21, 2012. Mother wanted this corrected and was proud of the accomplishment.

I changed the format, moved some things, reduced the page count, added a few pictures and lost the careful layout of trying to have the key pages always start on the right to free more space for 'more of mother', when I reprint.

You are getting all of mother's words.

The evolution of this book began on Valentine's Day 2011 in mother's apartment with a hand-held red voice recorder. I took the cover picture that day. (the picture on the front cover) It took several more visits with recorder in hand, and regular telephone calls to get what that day became known as--'her story, words and life in vignette.' I wasn't going to get more. That was the day the title was born.

It took some time to gather birthday comments, transcribe the audio, deal with day-to-day life, including mother having at the time very serious ulcer wounds, and wheelchair dilemma.

On August 28, 2011, I wrote the epilogue--the next day August 29th, the tribute poem 'She's Not Confined'. It was the day I got out of my way and could get down to the business of actually getting it done.

I had several copies printed for her birthday, October 9th. It was almost done. October 27, 2011, I finished. Mother proofread with me every word. Copies were printed. The book was such a help in letting the numerous medical intervention personnel know her after her horrible accident April 23, 2012, when she couldn't speak for herself. There were several update reprints.

Acknowledgments

Mother's memory, words and literal description of her life, enabled me to write this book. Without her active and accessible knowledge, my words couldn't adequately do it. I am grateful to be able to help her share with you--her life!

It has taken much to be able to include the sentiment and documentation for this book, to be offered as a small token of acknowledgement, and testimony to her life--and to have it ready in time for her birthday!

My Uncle Paul, and Aunt Betty, provided oral history. The Columbia, Missouri community has and continues to contribute memories, praise and compliments to their "Grandma Janet."

Dr. Michael Acuff's words were a beacon of light to mother, in her quest for health and medical awareness. She continued to constantly study and learn more about staying healthy.

Friends have stepped up to help me create and present a finished product--one good enough to share. This included photo help, formatting assistance, proofing--trying to catch typos, blatant grammar problems, and more. In the hurry for completion--there was not enough time, but I believe getting it done trumps forever saying "yes, but ..."

I thank each and every-one of you who has shared in word, comment, deed, and support to help me complete the first edition as a private printing for mother's 83rd birthday, October 9, 2011.

Quadriplegic quad•ri•ple•gic

Definition: Tetraplegia, also known as quadriplegia, is paralysis caused by illness or injury to a human that results in the partial or total loss of use of all their limbs and torso; Paraplegia is similar but does not affect the arms.

Michael Acuff, MD: Janet Barnes has incomplete tetraplegia. So that means she has some use of her arms and hands that's limited, and she has at least some feeling in her legs. She has a little bit of movement, so that is called incomplete tetraplegia or incomplete quadriplegia.

Angela: How does that differ from a complete quadriplegic?

Dr. Acuff: When a person has complete quadriplegia, then they have no feeling or movement below their chest. They won't have any feeling or movement in their legs.

Angela: Would someone be able to use their arms or move their hands?

Dr. Acuff: They would be able to use their arms and hands depending on the level of the quadriplegia, but they would not be able to move their legs.

Angela: Does this diagnosis in some way communicate to us she is not a quadriplegic?

No. She's quadriplegic without a doubt, because of her weakness and the limited use that she has of her hands, and because of the location where she had her injury in her neck. This makes her quadriplegic.

Vignettes

Vignette is a 3rd person singular present, plural of vignette.

Noun: A brief evocative description, account, or episode.

Verb: Portray (someone) in the style of a vignette. A short piece of writing, music, acting, etc. which clearly expresses the typical characteristics of something or someone.

Definition: A vignette is a style of a photograph whose edges fade out gradually to white or black. Vignetting can be an unintentional result caused by optical limitations in the camera lens. As an effect, it is frequently used for portrait photos, usually in an oval or other shape. A vignette effect is easy to apply to a digital photo in most photo-editing programs.

Dear Angela,

I'm glad you are writing a book about your mom!

I remember seeing her around Columbia through the years and wondering who she was and if I'd ever meet her as a patient. When I met her I realized why I hadn't met her as a patient sooner, she doesn't need a doctor!

I have enjoyed being her doctor through the years now, mostly because she has a healthy outlook on life and she helps me remember what is important in life. She stands up for her own rights, but she doesn't think that she is better or more important than anyone else! I have learned from her how I can be healthy!

Thank you.

Michael Acuff MD
Rusk Rehabilitation
Columbia, MO

She's Not

she's older, frailer
and sometimes discarded
but inside her is no age

inside her no boundary
just the outside
hampered, labored

but if you could see the spark
the heart, the joy, the glean
the eyes, the beliefs

the things she wanted to do
the things she would have done
the things she could inside her being do

and at times when her mind wasn't confined
there she lived full--free
with all of what she wanted inside to be

those were some of the times I didn't like
they scared the hell out of me
she took a break emotionally

I didn't yet know the confinement, the bondage
the hostage position that so often presented its jail bars
in reality right there with her

a curb she couldn't master--stuck
a shelf she couldn't reach, a jar she couldn't open
clothing she couldn't put on

Confined

cold--blizzardy
out in the weather, in all elements
arms and hands turning purple in the cold

beaten down with rain
moving with that tiny little frame
reaching just what she could reach

but out of body, out of mind's confinement--free
no wonder she longed to escape
and enjoyed those respites from reality

she's not confined
she is life defined
bold, courageous

she'd led the trail, not fallen behind
she's won the prize, defined the prize
she is the prize

I know of no mortal person
who could survive, thrive, and triumph her life
my mother, Janet Barnes, a 90-pound heavyweight

August 29, 2011

GIFTS

I got to know more of mother through the eyes and hearts of those she has touched, and by listening with my heart to her words.

I dedicate this book as my birthday gift to mother (as well as to all who will be inspired by her life), in recognition of her long, creative and productive life.

A life that has made an indelible impression on those she has met along the journey of life--me too.

My Mother

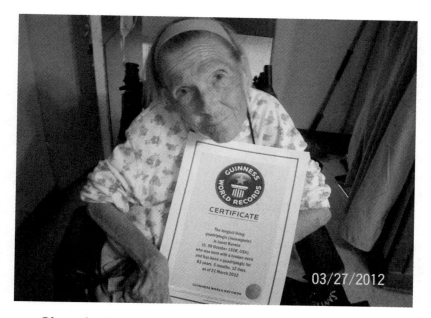

03/27/2012

Okay, this is my opportunity to introduce to you my mother, Janet Ernestine (Strong) Barnes, a 90-pound heavyweight. My recent task has been to transcribe her words literally--her sharing of her life. She wants to be heard. She deserves to be known.

This story is as unique as is she. She is literally the longest living quadriplegic, and also the oldest living, since her quadriplegia and birth were the same date, October 9th, 1928. Mother's medical definition is C5 (5th cervical) motor incomplete Tetraplegia, and that equals quadriplegia. She does have some movement, but the clinical definition remains 'quadriplegic'.

I am the oldest daughter, and writing this book has reminded me, and changed me--in more ways than I expected. The challenge was great--the prize and gifts greater.

As I am writing this, you right this moment, are seeing the first words that came to mind and paper, in the exact moment they are born. I ask you to open your eyes, ears, and heart, and get to know the life and triumph of this difficult and remarkable woman. I will do my best to present a reality based, although emotionally laden and challenging project.

Both my parents have been a hard act to follow. My dad, Harold Eugene Barnes, was born January 23, 1923 with two dislocated hips, and due to a series of family circumstances lived, and grew up at Missouri Baptist Hospital in St. Louis, Missouri. The teaching hospital used him for experimental practices, including surgeries. By the time he left the hospital, he lived his entire life in a wheelchair, and I don't mean the electric models or even the aluminum ones. For many years he pulled his heavy cane chair up the steps behind him. He wheeled the chair with raw, bleeding hands, and did whatever was needed to survive.

Daddy would give you the shirt off his back, and do anything and everything he could for everyone. If something was impossible he would literally say "it might take me a little longer."

Mother and Daddy both are/were the most initiatively talented, creative and courageous hard workers I have ever known. Mother could manage and make "enough" out of almost nothing. Their extremely limited financial resources stretched, and provided enough for four children. My perception is that we were nourished, physical needs met, and a variety of wants were also provided. Emotionally, life with mother was not easy.

Her mother and father, my grandparents, were not equipped or mature enough to be parents. I'm grateful that the grandmother I knew was the one my daughters were able to know.

My grandmother, whom I called Zaumie, was the best example of unconditional love I could experience. My sister, brothers, and I knew a consistent presence of support, enthusiasm, and day-to-day involvement from Zaumie and Moman. Moman joined our lives when I was very young. I remember Zaumie coming down the street with an accordion strapped onto her. It looked almost as big as she was. She was playing and kids were following her home. It was like she was a pied piper coming to us. For many years she lived near to us, and came over frequently to do whatever she could, especially to help mother.

Mother has made an indelible impression on so many, and in so many positive ways. I'll let her story show you, and you can decide for yourself if you know of anyone with more ability, determination and independence than this woman who couldn't move her feet, get in or out of bed unattended, reach to scratch an itch, or do most of the things we take for granted each and every day.

Mother was born at home, October 9th, 1928 at 8:00 a.m., in Mt. Vernon, Illinois. She was born with a broken neck. A teacher, Miss Eloise Wood, got her a pair of crutches, and taught her to walk with them when she was in first grade.

Before that, she was mostly left in bed, or put outside for the day to bake in the hot sun or ... She could not move to get up, dress, prepare food or even go to the bathroom.

You will hear mother describe vividly her memories, beliefs, opinions. She knows her facts. I know a lot, too. Ultimately you will get to know her determination, and ability to survive life, in an almost unlivable and intolerable series of realities--far more than just circumstances. Most giants would fail if presented the challenges that have been her normal life. I am proud of her. She survived, thrived and made a difference in many, many lives.

I continue to know and learn more of this as I receive comments, cards, and memory sharing from the people whose lives and hearts she has touched.

So, I guess I am attempting to show you another side of life, thrived and survived, by a ninety-pound, physically frail woman, who pushed the envelope and mastered her universe from an electric wheelchair that weighed more than three times her weight--a chair that has literally been dumped over on her!

Initial Tape Recording

A: (Angela) It's your turn to talk. We're recording.

J: (Janet) Okay, ready for recording.

A: We need to be recording it now.

J: Okay.

A: Try it for a few minutes...

J: Am I close enough to do it?

A: I don't know. We're going to test that now.

J: All right. Okay. Now can I stop?

A: Talk to it!

J: I don't know what to say to it.

A: Say some more anyway.

J: *It's an awful little bitty thing to talk to.*

A: It's recording.

J: That means it's recording when it's on red--right?

A: Yes. You just keep speaking. You tell your story--talk.

J: I'm 82 years old now. Well, I like to live. I kind of live by 'sayings'. "An ounce of prevention is worth a pound of cure." "Anyone who thinks he's hot stuff is definitely cool crap." All kinds of sayings--more sayings.

A: Well, you fill it up with more, and then we stop.

May You Experience

Enough happiness to be content
Enough discontent to progress
Enough incentive to grow into maturity
Enough maturity to deserve respect
Enough self-confidence to banish fear
Enough problems to develop an active mind
Enough accomplishments to feel secure
Enough lack of ability to keep you humble
Enough humility to be thoughtful of others
Enough health and peace to have memory
Enough memory to retain knowledge
Enough knowledge to choose intelligently
Enough consciousness to know right from wrong
Enough self-discipline to do what's right
Enough basis of comparison to judge wisely
Enough ideals to work hard for justice
Enough determination to achieve goals
Enough optimism to see good in everything
Enough inner peace to keep you strong
Enough success to keep you encouraged
Enough friends to deter feeling alone
Enough gratitude to be deserving
Enough ability and income to be independent
Enough enthusiasm to enjoy a great life
Enough understanding to eliminate anger
Enough appreciation of having enough

Experienced and prepared by Janet Barnes 1998

Life Before Daddy

Paul (uncle and playmate), Donny,
Stewart (brothers) and Mother

Mother age 9 and 14

Paintings

The top picture has a little water running over the rocks. I made it when I was sixteen. I just looked at a picture and I painted it. I had to prepare the canvas. I put the backing on it, and made the frame and then wrapped the canvas around it. I painted a yellow tree, orange tree, a green tree and a brown tree, and water running over the rocks.

The bottom picture I did when I was seventeen. It has a little walk or driveway and trees and a house. Both of these were done when I was in high school. Miss Randall was a pretty good artist (mother's only high school teacher all four years, and lifetime friend).

Now, how do I turn it off?

Stop.

First Grade On

In first grade, Miss Eloise Woods came to my home in Mt. Vernon. (Illinois)

Mother wrote the Board of Education, and got them to send a teacher to the house for me. I lived with my maternal grandmother in Mt. Vernon pretty much. We got along real well.

In the second grade, my teacher was Florence Daugherty, and Mr. Erwin drove me and Maureen Coffee to her home.

In the third grade, Mr. Erwin took three of us to Mini Bee Turrentine's--Jackie Williams, Lois Cooley, and me. Fourth grade was the same.

In the fifth grade, we all went to Horace Mann School. It was Jackie, Lois, me and Ansel Burwell, and another guy, but he was on crutches.

Dickey Buffy took me out for New Year's Eve and brought me home at 10 p.m.

Daddy, my dad, was already working in St. Louis, and I stayed at Mom Collins. (Maternal grandmother)

I moved to St. Louis when I was eleven. We lived on the 2nd and 3rd floors. It was really hard for me.

I started Elias Michael School in St. Louis when I was eleven.

Classmates: Rosie Schwartz; Jules Freeman--he had cerebral palsy, and was so smart; David Jackman--I stopped him from choking to death one day.

I met Betty McFarland and we were going to adopt kids, but you had to be married, so we were going to get rid of our husbands and raise children together. Betty and I were very close. Lizbeth Jane McFarland. I called her Liza Jane. She went to live with her uncle in California. She was from around Farmington, Missouri. Her brother was in the Navy, but I could never locate her.

I was at Elias Michael (school) seven years. It was a good school.

Verna (classmate) was a flirt. She ran after Paul. We met the President (Roosevelt). We were autograph hounds. We waited to meet Errol Flynn. They wouldn't let us, but we did meet two soldier boys at President Roosevelt's birthday ball. They had it at the Kiel. Mother worked there and I got to go for free.

We had school picnics. It took me six years to get mother to go to a picnic. She didn't like to be around wheelchairs. After she went to one, she liked it so good she went all the time.

Mother and Folks Drinking

J: I don't know if you want this in here or not.

A: I'm going to type everything.

Well, I had the most lack of responsible parents. The folks went out to taverns most of the time, and the taverns didn't close until two in the morning.

I would lay awake always until like 2:00 a.m. in the morning. It was easier to wait for them in the morning till they sobered up, when I knew they were there, than when I didn't know where they were. So, I spent my whole life waiting to make sure they got home, and then until they sobered up enough to come and get me up.

At one time, my dad came to get me after midnight. They'd have a drunken party, and I wasn't allowed to go onto the living room rug--the rug that all those drunks could burp up all over, and dance all over it. And I didn't get mad because people don't want to be wrong on purpose, this is for sure. Everybody is doing as well as they can with what they have to work with. Lots of people don't have much to work with.

One time my folks didn't come back the next day, and they didn't come back the next. They came back the following morning. I was all alone all that time. Donny got up and fixed breakfast, but I could not eat anything lying in bed. I've had a life of being all anxious. I mean really, really anxious. But the reason I wouldn't let mother wait till she got out of the hospital to get a watch was so she would know right then--so she didn't have to lay and wonder what time it was.

Mother was referring to my grandmother having had open-heart surgery and later a stroke that cost her most of her vision...

I Had a Goat

I carried home a goat that Brother Wadell (Mom Collin's minister) gave me. I carried him in my lap, and Paul pushed me and the goat home in a wheelbarrel.

My dad fed the goat tailor-made cigarettes, ones like Lucky Strike, and things like that. I hand rolled the others.

The goat didn't care which cigarettes it ate, but my dad would give him the tailor-made ones, and mother didn't like that. The goat was named 'Pet'.

We also had a cow that lived in the back yard, and Saturday nights she would come around, and put her feet on the porch steps, and listen to the barn dance music on the radio.

Donny and Stewart (brothers) thought I was the most special thing that ever was, and they really cared about me. They always just called me Sis. They may not even of known my name.

My dad and Dad Strong worked at the railroad place that made train wheels, and it was so hot that they would burn their hands if they took their pocket watch out of their pocket without having gloves on.

Work

When I was ten to twelve, I painted pictures on glasses (glassware) to double my money. I bought my own clothes.

Between twelve and fourteen dad made me bracelets, and I etched monograms by painting on the part that wasn't to be painted with black tar paint. I'd put them in muriatic acid, and that way it etched what wasn't painted. I gave them for gifts or sold them. Those two years I had sores in my nose, 'cause muriatic acid made sores.

> Muriatic acid is an aqueous solution of hydrogen chloride gas (HCl). It is a highly corrosive acid.

Sixteen and seventeen, besides going with Tootie, I worked at Goodwill 35 hours a week.

At eighteen I graduated from the Gerhart School of Photography. Vocational Rehab sent me there. I always liked pretty things. Thurston (tenant) became a photographer and a retoucher.

I worked 24 years retouching films. I paid my own social security. I've been a busy person, and I read everything. I still have 20/20 vision. Let me tell you how I do that. I started taking bilberry to keep the veins open, and I take vision formula to give them everything they need.

I'm having trouble now because I'm in so much sun and it burns. The other day it was raining so much the drops were in my eyes. I stopped at a Laundromat and tried to get dry. Boy did I get wet. I got so wet my wheelchair was squeaking.

Bicycle and Training Wheels

J: I rode my bicycle from my maternal grandmother's house up to my paternal grandmother's house in Mt Vernon. (Illinois) I stayed with my maternal grandmother Mom Collins a lot.

A: What about the bike?

J: I had to buy training wheels to see if I could balance. I rode the bike when the wheels were off the ground. One day my dad took the wheels off, went around behind me, and it was a lot easier. I went with him back and forth.

A: Well, how did you design it and get them made?

J: I drew it on graphic paper. I went to St. Louis and told the engineer at Guarantee Cycle on Olive Street what I wanted. He told me it would cost $40.00 for my training wheels, and $40.00 for my bike. I rode it quite easily.

I invented the wheels because Dr. Franklin told my folks that I wouldn't live past fourteen, because of lack of balance. I was told that when I was eleven, and that is when they left me at Shiner's Hospital in St. Louis. They were supposed to leave me at eight, but they thought I wouldn't live past fourteen. I thought he meant equilibrium. He meant biochemical. I think he was real smart to know that. I wouldn't want the biochemical of an athlete, because they think they're hot stuff, and anybody who thinks they are hot stuff is definitely cool crap. That's one of my sayings.

I was seventeen when I invented and designed the training wheels. Mine didn't stay on the ground. I moved it a bit higher off the ground, so I rode the bike just on its two wheels.

Tootie

I told you one time of a sailor boy. His name was Hugh Leroy Bain. Hugh means "intelligent spirit". His baby brother named Ronald, called him 'Tootie'. He wrote me three times a day. He sent me gifts from everywhere.

I went with him for a year between sixteen and seventeen. He asked my aunt if he could marry me. I told him, he was supposed to ask me first.

I didn't marry him. He was as good as he could be, and he loved me. He never told me he loved me. He said "You're a nut, and I like nuts." The reason I didn't marry him was because I didn't think his mother would let him marry me, and I would rather him be upset with me than his mother. He lived across the street from me.

I Never Worried Mother

I didn't worry mother ever, but I worked all day to keep Harold from getting a chance to ask me to take his ring. I went to the Empress Theatre, and mother didn't know where I was. It worried her, and Thurston came and found me and walked me home. He lived in our upstairs apartment.

His name was William Baker Thurston. William means 'protector'. I addressed him by his last name, Thurston.

Thurston and Harold showed up about three days apart. I cared about both of them. I respond to need. Harold had greater need.

Nothing ever stopped us.
There was nothing beyond determination.

Your daddy wanted kids and I wanted to give
him boys and girls. I would have felt like
a failure without giving him both.

Life With Daddy

Daddy Didn't Have Anything

Lorene, daddy's sister, didn't know he had more problems than I did. She fussed because my parents let him marry me. He didn't have anybody or anything. He worked from fifteen to twenty-two at the switchboard. He'd taken care of it since he was nine years old. When whoever was working wanted to have a day off, he'd say, "I'll take over the board." Then when he asked for a $5.00 a month raise and they told him "no", he left. I'd only met him a few days before. He had no place to go and nothing to eat. I was already working and had enough to pay for a room.

Dr. Kline was sponsoring daddy at the hospital until he died. Daddy's dad had died.

Due to a series of family circumstances, he was raised as an orphan at Missouri Baptist Hospital. They did thirteen experimental surgeries on him. He had sore throats constantly. He was as good as he could be, and he needed help. All I do is to respond to need. If I find somebody who needs somebody--I respond.

He had only a 4th grade tangible education, and he didn't have a lot going for him. He had to hustle--he'd always had to hustle. I don't like it when people have to hustle--that's rough.

I Met Your Daddy

I met your daddy when he was twenty-two. I was eighteen or nineteen. I married him when I was twenty. I was down the hill on the sidewalk on my bicycle. He was wheeling up the hill in his wheelchair. He came up and we sat on the steps and talked.

We (mother's family) rented an apartment at 3815 Westminster, on the first floor, but it had fourteen steps to get up from the outside. Harold gave me a little cocker spaniel, Golden Eclipse, and I took that dog up the fourteen steps on a leash.

We didn't make enough money for a car, so we got a scooter. It didn't look good and it didn't turn much. I bought him a motorette, and the motorette wouldn't take me up any hills. I had to walk up (walked with crutches and brace) the hills to our house. It wouldn't go over hills with two of us. Then we got a scooter and a side-car, and we already had you (Angela), but you wouldn't ride in the side-car, and the dog wouldn't ride in the side-car, but the dog would follow daddy every time he left. He'd pick him up somehow and get him back home. We went to Mt. Vernon with the scooter and side-car, and I got burned up going down, and bugs were in my face coming back.

Did you get all of that?

Married By a Minister

I had already graduated from high school and photo retouching school. I worked at home and made about a dollar an hour. I was working enough to pay for a room and we could get an apartment for $39.00 a month, so I married him.

Your daddy was not well. I thought he was going to die. I thought he had cancer. He burped up blood and passed blood all the time. I didn't know if he'd live for a day, a week, or a month.

I wouldn't take his ring (Harold's) forever and ever. He won it in a poker game and tried to get me to take it home. It was leap year day, which was February 29 (that would have been 1948), but I didn't take it because that's when a girl asks a boy. I married him the next day after leap year, January 1st, 1949.

You were born two weeks before I was twenty-one. I got married when I was twenty and because you were born eight months and twenty-five days after we were married, Mom Collins, my grandmother, said I had to marry your daddy.

We got weighed on top of the court house steps after we had our marriage license. We both weighed 107 pounds.

Rev. Cleo Flannigan married us in the back of a panel truck. This thing was like a closed in van--no windows.

If I had been the groom, I wouldn't want to be sitting down while my bride stood. The van had a bench going length-wise and Harold, and the minister and I sat on the bench, and our witnesses, Paul and Helen, my uncle and his wife, sat in the front two seats. So we all sat down for our wedding.

I wore a yellow flannel shirt (I think mother corrected me and said yellow sweat shirt) and blue jeans. Blue jeans were a symbol of independence. Mother never let me wear blue jeans. Daddy was all dressed up. We babysat on our honeymoon, and took care of John's (uncle) kids, and they were difficult. My goodness, they marked the mirrors and windows with lipstick.

Wedding Vow

My vow was silent, and I didn't tell anybody till about four or five years ago. (around 2007)

I don't pray to ask for anything. Nobody has ever done a better vow.

I wanted to be able to give Harold all that any other man could have, and try to make up for the pain and unhappiness he had lived through, and to let whatever he could come up with, or be able to make, be enough. I didn't know if he'd live long enough for me to do all that.

"I did that"

I did pray for someone to love, and be loved by.

I was so alone.

First Baby

Grandmother, Mother, Great-grandmother and Angela

When they couldn't find Dr. Antsee, and I went into labor at 7:00 p.m. on September 25th, they put me in the hospital. Dr. Walther was really upset. He was going crazy because he couldn't get an operating room because they were all being used, and you were scheduled for a C-Section. I never made a sound 'cause doctors can't stand a woman screaming. I never told your daddy there was any pain involved. He wasn't even there when you were born. He was taking Rosie (mother's friend and later my god-mother) to get a job. I got you in three hours and ten minutes, and that's really fast for a first baby. I never was a baby about nothing.

A: You think it helped because of your swinging on crutches, and riding on a bike? Is that why you didn't need a C-Section?

J: Yes. Yes. And also, I didn't want to worry your daddy and he would have worried bad, if I took a long time. I never would have told him there was any pain involved.

Houses

A: I remember living on Penrose.

J: Harold gave me an apple tree, and he grew me a rose garden. We grew tomatoes.

A: What about Penrose? Did you have to remodel there?

J: Yes. We had to do everything. We had to put the bathroom in. We didn't have a bathroom. The bathroom was on the second floor.

We had a dog named 'Something'. That dog high-tailed over the fence and tried to get out and we'd go up and down the street and holler, "Here Something, here Something."

A Who sold you the house on Penrose? Was it Mr. Burkhoff, and was it his wife who gave us gingerbread houses?

J: No. That was the Yaley's. Yaley's were friend of... They gave us clothes for you and a gingerbread house. My folks didn't do much on clothes even when I was little. My folks basically bought beer, some whiskey and cigarettes.

A: So, College is the remodeling I know. (family home)

J: Yes. Daddy lowered the ceilings. We put in the windows, poured the concrete floor in the basement, and made the sidewalks. The only time that daddy cussed was when he was downstairs working on fixing the electric dryer. It didn't have an automatic start, and the electric sparked. He got shocked and broke his finger. I heard him cuss. He worked at the switchboard with a broken finger for six weeks.

The Family Grew

Brian Michael, Janet Angela Mary, Robyn Lynn and
Harold Eugene Jr. (Gene) Barnes

The Kids Too

Dogs

We raised Basset Hounds for five years. I had forty-one dogs to find places for when daddy died. I put the bassets in the kennels, and I got puppies for two years. They sold them and gave me money for them. I gave the Chihuahuas to special people. One woman said she'd give me a Boston-Bull terrier, and I picked a Beagle.

What we raised professionally were Chihuahua's and Beagles. One night, on Harold's birthday, Lynn (the female dog) produced twelve puppies. Harold would feed six, and she'd feed six. They raised those pups together.

Raising dogs was quite a job for us, and we made more money with this than both of our social security checks together.

We couldn't get a fifth child so we raised dogs instead--like our babies.

Marsianna, born April 14th. Aries and Mars is a guiding name. I called her Marsi. She was a personal pet and just a beautiful dog--really good.

We got Frodo from the human society. We found the doctor who had taken him to Humane Society, and we learned the name he had given. We named him Frodo. He was a natural born rabbit hunter.

Life

We bought a lot at Goose Creek, and then they put all the sand in, and we couldn't get to it (the beach area). We'd go down on weekends. We made a shed, we'd cook and sleep in the station wagon.

We had a pool in the yard. We dug down and put in an 8' round tub, and two 10" high concrete blocks. That gave us corners to sit in and 4' of water.

We had a very good life.

I had as good a life as anybody could ever have, anywhere. I did a lot more than a lot of able-bodied people could. I would not have been happy if I hadn't gotten your daddy boys and girls. When I was twenty-seven I told him I'd give him a son for his thirtieth birthday and I missed by eleven days.

I've studied all cultures. Hindus are honest. Muslims are so truthful they do not have to take an oath in court. The reason they can have up to four wives is because there is no welfare system. They can have all they can afford.

I've studied all faiths, and all names. Every name has a meaning. I studied astrology when I was seventeen. Aquarius was my most compatible. Daddy was an Aquarian.

Harold never left me in bed--never! No matter what shift he worked, he got me up so I could take care of the kids. My folks always left me in bed.

Mother After I Had Kids

Mother was real happy to have you (referring to me, Angela.) Fussed about me getting you--but she was good to you after I had you.

Moman (the man who was my grandfather by love, presence, and availability) was good for mother. She quit drinking for him. He wouldn't let her drink because he'd had another wife that was a drunk.

When she lived on Lee Avenue, we were just back of her, on Penrose, a couple doors down. You walked from Penrose to Holy Rosary. It was a long walk. (I went to kindergarten at Holy Rosary School.)

We always took you guys to the basement for tornados.

She sure got along with Moman better than she did my dad.

She always made spaghetti, and spaghetti was so hard for me to eat. She and Donny liked spaghetti. Me and dad liked pork 'n beans and fried potatoes. I think she made meatloaf quite a bit too.

She had a fit each time I got pregnant, but she liked the kids. She provided transportation.

She quit drinking when she was fifty, and quit smoking at eighty. She was very cross when she was quitting smoking. I offered to buy her anything she wanted but she went cold turkey.

She did a good job to live to be eighty-six. She took strong vitamins.

Moman was good, but Moman had to always be right, whether he was right or not. He got a lot of speeding tickets. He always had to be first. Moman did not drink.

He rode a motorcycle and she wouldn't ride a motorcycle with him. Moman was good to you kids.

She was good to you guys too. She was really happy to have you. She over-did everything quite a bit. They settled down to be pretty good people when they got older. By the time you guys got here.

My dad and Louise (dad's second wife) got along real good--they got along fine. My mother and my dad never got along--they drank.

She moved on College (same street as our house) to be closer. I went down once when we were getting robbed by people. Frodo, named Furocious Frodo, (the dog) took the man's wrist that was trying to take things out from under the Christmas tree and took him out of the house.

Harold Barnes: Independent Operator

Alexian Brothers Hospital Newspaper
ECHO Vol 3 No 2 Nov 1972

To an anxious caller, Harold Barnes is a reassuring and calm voice on the ABH switchboard. To the hospital's 520 employees, Harold is an efficient operator, cheerfully transferring calls, paging people, and assisting in any way possible.

While Harold's skills at the switchboard are well known, not everyone knows that these same deft fingers can also remodel a house and rebuild a car. For anyone, these would be accomplishments... for a man in a wheelchair, they might be thought impossible. But nothing daunts Harold. At the age of three he contracted polio and spent most of the next 15 years at Missouri Baptist Hospital, undergoing 13 operations.

What Harold can accomplish from a wheelchair would make many able-bodied men envious. His seven-room home in north St. Louis is a former store which he remodeled himself, building scaffolding and crawling to it from the floor. Everything is on one level: the sliding doors are extra wide and the light switches are low. With a textbook as a constant companion, Harold installed plumbing and wiring and created a custom-made kitchen for his

wife Janet, who is also confined to a wheelchair most of the time after contracting what doctors think was a combination of polio and cerebral palsy.

Harold Barnes is a man of many facets, only one of which is operating the busy ABH switchboard.

Harold drives his own car, a '64 Chevy wagon for which he made manual controls. The mass produced hand controls didn't suit him. "And I make better ones myself." says Harold, and he did.

Married 30 Years and 5 Months

I called the hospital, and they found him with no heartbeat. They asked, "Can I take it? I said, "What else, can I do?" Daddy died May 16, 1979.

Harold finally got fairly healthy. We were married 30 years and 5 months. He had a pace maker. They (hospital) drowned him. We had about 25 years of him being comparatively healthy, and the last five he had heart attacks.

I was 50 and he was about 54-1/2. We had a very contented life. We didn't quarrel. We had four kids before you were six. We didn't have time to argue.

He didn't wash any dishes until after I cracked up (nervous breakdown). I didn't marry him for money or to buy me things. I married him to give him a life, and that isn't what girls usually do.

Mr. Warmen, mother's boyfriend, fussed about Harold not giving me an engagement ring. But Harold won my engagement ring in a poker game, and my wedding band we got for $13.00 at a pawn shop. It had five diamond chips, so I wanted a fifth baby.

Daddy was a gambler--probably always was, but he had the worst luck, and I only respond to need--never to greed-- just need. Every time he played with my uncles, he lost. He quit gambling, and said he was lucky at love.

We were legally married and supporting ourselves. My husband and I both knew we were equal. All we had to do to retain the other's respect and interest was be ourselves. There is no hating in me.

I would not trade places with anybody.
I've learned more than anybody could ever learn.
That's for sure.

I'm eighty-two.
Quadriplegics do not live that long!

Life After Daddy

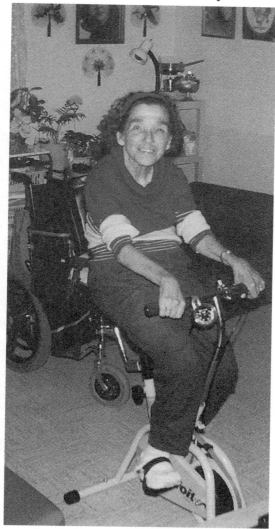

When I saw this little exerciser in the store I said
"What size child does this exerciser fit?"
I said, "I want it. It fits me and my apartment."

Triple Pet Net and Crochet Dolls

I didn't have any stuffed animals at all until after daddy died. My aunt made me an oil cloth Scotty dog when I was little, and somewhere along the way a little rabbit. I gathered these up since I came here. (moved to Columbia MO after daddy died) I've got all kinds of stuff represented. I have a knitted 'triple pet net' and that's something very special. I probably am the only one in the world with a triple pet net.

A: Mother, what about the crochet dolls you made?

J: Over to your right.

A: I don't know who made that little pink doll there. Did you?

J: No.

A: You made that beautiful rainbow one for Tiffany.
(granddaughter)

J: My maternal grandmother taught me to crochet left handed when I was eight or nine. I wrapped the yarn around my good hand...

Mother doesn't have a good hand.

WEATHER--Hot, Cold, Rain and Snow

It is said that as many days as there are in the whole journey, so many are the men and horses that stand along the road, each horse and man at the interval of a day's journey; and these are stayed neither by snow nor rain nor heat nor darkness from accomplishing ttheir appointed course with all speed.

(A.D. Godley 1924)

We are mothers and fathers, and sons and daughters. Who every day go about our lives with duty, honor and pride. And neither snow, nor rain, nor heat, nor gloom of night, nor the winds of change, nor a nation challenged, will stay us from the swift completion of our appointed rounds. Ever.

http://en.wikipedia.org/wiki/United_States_Postal_Service_creed

J: No, no.   One time this man looked at me and Tammy (granddaughter). It was so cold. I was so stiff like a corpse. She had trouble getting me in the car. When I get cold, I get stiff.

Cold weather--I don't run around as much in cold weather. I can take any heat, even 107--anything. I get a lot of vitamin D. Cold weather freezes me. I run around in sweat shirts. My hands get cold. I get a scarf wrapped around my neck and sometimes I wear a mitten on my left hand. I've been stuck in the snow. I'm safer on ice than anybody walking. I slide a little bit, but in a chair, you don't break your leg. Well, I don't get out if I can't make it, or if the snow banks are too big. I can get around pretty good in snow.

Construction and cars can block the road. Sometimes I'll get on one end, and can't get off the other, so I have to go back because it's too steep. I go back where I got on, and sometimes you can't get up and down. It's scary to go up in a chair.

The sun doesn't bother me like the cold. My folks put me out in the shade in the morning, and let me get cooked all day, and brought me inside in the evening. I baked in the sun.

I never threw a dish, never hollered, never cussed--just waited. No one could have heard me anyway. I didn't have enough voice out in the sun. I just waited.

Anger is a non-constructive attitude. When I was little, it was the only thing that ever killed anybody--don't get angry, and don't eat salt. I never ate salt, and never got angry.

How I kept from getting angry. The way I don't be angry is in knowing that no one is wrong on purpose, everyone is doing as good as they can with what they have to work with. Some people don't have much to work with. All I was ever taught I learned by reverse psychology. I learned to be responsible, and to accept responsibility, and to provide.

My folks couldn't do that. They used all their money for parties on pay day.

In the rain I get wet, but I don't melt. I always carry a poncho to get put on me. I never leave home without a cell phone and a poncho.

Rain hits me in the eyes like little pin points and it bangs me in the eyes. I still have 20/20 vision and I can hear when the rain starts to drip on the roof.

My chair needs a bag over the control knobs in rain.

I got lost once, and couldn't find my way home. I really got lost, and I was getting colder and colder. I went into a hotel with an automatic open door, and I asked the man there to put me in front of the heater to get me warm. This is where I asked him if he would look up about the woman recognized as the oldest living quad. He went and printed out me three pages. I lost the papers, but I know I am the oldest living quad.

Computer Programmer

A: After daddy died, you went to computer school?

J: Yes, I came here. (Freedom House)I'm a computer programmer. Everybody should be one. It teaches you to be a problem solver. In fact--you don't sleep at night. You satisfy your specs. You're expected to make the problem work. You do that all night long. You don't sleep when you're a computer programmer. When I was working there (Todkomp), you think it all out. Everybody should take it because you get to be a problem solver, real good.

A: What did you get trained in?

J: Computer programming! You do whatever the problem is. You have to make it work.

A: What are the languages that you took?

J: BASIC and Cobalt were the ones I was working with.

A: You had to live somewhere else while you were studying. You didn't commute, right?

J: I was here. (Freedom House) Oh, I was living at Todkomp...

A: Was this where you took the classes?

J: Yes.

A: So, they had a residential facility?

J: Yeah, yeah, for a while. And then I came here, and I didn't graduate. They were not going to let an older woman take a man's job. I would have passed, but he gave me a program with two files, and nobody else had done that. He said, "I don't know if you will ever get this." So, I put myself into the Career Center, and I graduated from there. Let me show you my certificate. Right here--Certificate of Completion. See right there--A+ Average. I did a two- year course in one year there. I lived at Todkomp for about a year, and I moved here to Freedom House the year it opened--think it was '82. It took me about a year to get things going.

Dumped Out of a Wheelchair, Dog Bite, and...

A: You got dumped out of your chair at different times.

J: And that time they took me to the hospital, and I was going to go to University Hospital, but then I realized I had to wheel myself back home. I had my shoulder broken then, and I said "NO--take me to Boone Hospital!" It was closer. It hurt like crazy. I also wacked my eye. That was worse. It was awful to look at me.

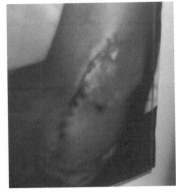

If you're scared of dogs you get jumpy. I wasn't scared of them, but that thing came up right behind me, and it went, "Ruff," and went on past me, and was facing me. It came back real fast, and grabbed my arm, and bit it all the way to the bone. Then it went into its house. I've been accused of hearing voices. I've never heard voices before, but boy, this voice said, "See what house that dog goes into, and get yourself to the hospital." I never got into any trouble listening to that voice. I had to wheel about three miles to the hospital. All the flesh and blood was hanging out, bleeding all over the sidewalk, and uh, I got to the hospital.

Highlights

A: So, I guess you're talking about highlights today. We can talk on the phone and get more later if you want. What topics?

J: I think we've about covered them! Now, I made candles. Look at that snowman in there. She (name withheld by author) gave me that Klondike horse and cart.

A: You have all kinds of souvenirs.

J: I made that snowman candle and I made another one over there if I can pick it out. Let me see what else I've got.

A: You've lived at this place for how many years?

J: About thirty years. (name withheld by author) gave me that little flower. I guess it's an azalea. He tried to get me azaleas forever. Azalea means all things in moderation.

A: Is there anything else you can think of that you wish you could have gotten off of your log that could help people or that you want to tell?

J: I still got my log up until two years ago. I can't get my computer on by myself because it got broke and the new one, I'm not managing.

A: Do we need to try to do it when I come back next time?

J: Yes...

A: Okay.

I Didn't Miss Much

A: Okay. I know about the horseback riding a little. What were you saying about quarter horses? Weren't they having you ride the horses when it was ridiculous? And I remember going to the swimming pool.

J: I went swimming with one of the schools--I think in the heated pool.

A: I remember you using fins and an inner tube.

J: I had the valves taken out of the inside and put on the outside to make me a swim tube. With the fins on my feet I could get around real good.

A: You stepped in the ocean too--on crutches. I don't understand that one. It was impossible, and you did it. Daddy couldn't get out there in a wheelchair.

J: Yes. I didn't walk very far out into the ocean--just a little bit.

A: We were pretty young kids, and you were walking in the ocean.

J: I was expecting Gene.

A: I have a picture somewhere of you going up and down the steps off Grand Avenue. What about the boat?

J: My second cousin and I went in a boat. I was in the back end.

I sat at the point end. He put me in first, and when he stepped down, I plopped out like a big fish, under the docks. He grabbed me by the left ankle. I told myself he could get me out.

I've bowled, but I couldn't hold the ball. They had it on a runner, and I bowled.

I'm very, very competitive, and everything I compete in I get a ribbon. In the games [Special Olympics], I got high toss. I had to move back with the high toss. I couldn't throw forward. I did the high toss backwards. And running around the track (in a wheelchair), I got a ribbon for that. All my ribbons are over there on the wall.

I've done about everything. I didn't miss much.

I didn't spell very good, because I was taught to be obedient, and you don't be obedient and spell right. I could never spell 'their' because that breaks the rule, and after you're spanked when you're 4-1/2 months old, you don't break rules. I was very special--really! I couldn't break rules. I had to give myself permission to break that rule before I could spell 'their', and I was already teaching at Shepard, before I got that far, because you can't break rules, you can't break rules, and you can't spell if you can't break rules, because you'd have to break rules all the time to spell right.

Aqua and Pink Snakeskin Shoes

I bought snakeskin tennis shoes from a catalog. They were aqua and pink like snake-skin. This is the only time I put myself first. I ordered them for $21.00, and I threw away the catalog. Everyone would look to see if they were real. And nobody knew where to get them. So I am the only one around here who has them.

When I volunteered at the Hospital, at least three people each day would reach down to see if they were real.

I have volunteered half of my life--forty-one years.

The reason for the snakeskin shoes was because we were talking to Mormons, (Church of Jesus Christ of Latter-day Saints) and they are really terrific. This one Mormon had a black velvet hat with a snakeskin band around the hat, and that was the prettiest thing I'd ever seen. I coveted that for your daddy. I always buy my shoes at 'wardrobe' (resale shop) for a dollar or sometimes a dollar-and-a- quarter.

Mother Talking...

J: Take a picture of Grandma and Grandpa with me, when I was 4-1/2 months old. (Picture is on her bedroom wall and you will see in the personal info section).

A: I don't know if it will take through the glass like this.

J: My great-grandfather is the one who took care of me 'till I was about four or five years old.

A: This one right here?

J: Um-hum. He taught me to count to 10 before I was twenty-two months old--and that's pretty special. It took brain power with me being born with a birth injury. I think it's because my folks just let me lay till I was 4-1/2 months. In a way, I couldn't continue developing. An old lady (name withheld by author) told my mother, there's something wrong with that baby, it's supposed to move, or it's supposed to cry. That's why my daddy spanked my baby bottom at 4-1/2 months old, and I never did forget that. I didn't remember too much about it until about three years ago.

That's the fourth generation with you in it over there.

A: I know. If you want to we can do the highlights by phone when I get home.

J: There's a thought that didn't come to me. I've always had the one where my daddy spanked me. Well--first about how much mother said she loved me, and then would reach down and bite me on the stomach.

Other thoughts. I never would have gone to bed with someone I wasn't married to, because I didn't want that kind of mess. That was it. So everything that happened to me--I made it make me stronger and better.

People at church said I was already pregnant when I married. I wasn't pregnant. We didn't even have sex before we got married. We did pet too heavy, but I understood why. Harold wanted children and he wanted to see if he thought I could have them. We didn't have sex.

I didn't tell on anybody. Mother had boyfriends. If she hadn't, I probably would have never had sex, because I thought it was the most painful thing in the world. Every time she and daddy had sex she screamed. I didn't ever want to have it if it's that much screaming. Oh my goodness--she had boyfriends. I couldn't stand her boyfriends.

When daddy was choking her to death, (she lived) I had already put in the phone for work. (Mother was doing telephone calling for Goodwill) I started to call the police. He took the phone out of the wall, and knocked me flat on the floor. So--I told on him to my paternal grandmother when I was sixteen, and she said, "Janet, be good to him. He'll always have to take care of you." That made me disgustedly independent.

I've always taken care of myself. I have physical limitations, but my mind is developed. I've probably got more wrinkles in my brain than anybody could ever have.

They (people) don't even think about it. One of my attendants moves her muscle before she thinks all the time. She knocked my whole computer off the table and tore it all up. She doesn't think before she moves! You can do an awful lot of damage if you don't think before you move.

I could even get shoes on little baby feet. None of you would hold your bottles. I had to hold bottles for everybody. I washed out between 14 and 21 diapers a day. I hand washed them out until after Christmas, and we got a little washing machine for your diapers.

We joined the Catholic Church because, well, for one thing, they were fairer than most churches. In my grandmother's church, if you put lipstick on you were condemned to hell. Smoke a cigarette, you were condemned to hell. There wasn't anything you couldn't do and not go to hell. Well, I already condemned everyone I knew to hell, so I definitely was not going to heaven. The Catholic Church was much fairer than some of them.

And do you know why the Catholics didn't eat meat on Friday? It was the bishop on an island where they had all kinds of fish, but no cows and stuff. You don't have cows and stuff on an island, and he couldn't get the people to eat the fish. They just used it for fertilizer. So, that's what stopped them from eating meat on Friday. They didn't eat it for their health. They had all kinds of fish and they were just throwing it away. I have to know the 'whys'. And for the 'why', that's sensible. It's alright to do it. If it's for survival, almost anything goes.

A: When did you start working at the hospital?

J: I volunteered there for twenty years, and I finished up about four or five years ago. I've been a foster grandparent for nineteen years. I was still at the hospital when I was a foster grandparent for a while. I was a courier at the hospital for twenty years. I don't know if the badge, 'ONE OF A KIND' came from there or the school.

A: You carried everything?

J: Yep, and when they stopped having babies over there, I didn't have as much to carry as I did when I was taking them to new mothers. I know the language of flowers. People's words have at least six meanings, and they don't all mean the same thing.

Now, 'perhaps' is different. 'Perhaps' means maybe and maybe means perhaps. But, I never liked any definition for love.

J: Well, daisies don't tell, and I don't believe in that. I think if it's there, it should be told, and out in the open. I don't believe in secrets.

A: I was thinking more about your reaction to the Gerber daisies, and still delivering them.

J: I worked all my life. It doesn't hurt anybody to work. I am living proof that I have taken good care of my body. It is everybody's responsibility to take care of their body.

I still eat with all my own teeth. They're all broke off from taking the large doses of potassium I was prescribed, and in my opinion, threatened into taking.

I am living proof that the person who realizes that they have to take care of their own body, and reads and researches and learns what to do, can keep themselves healthy.

For instance, when I had dry bones. I researched and learned what to take to make cartilage. I am still making cartilage. It is the cushioning between the bones.

I'm not on any medicine and I'm 83 and that's quite a feat.

One of the Best Times of My Life

Well, I think it was Blue Ridge (school) one year, and Shepard (school) for eighteen years. I was at Derby Ridge one summer. It had automatic doors. I liked that.

A little boy about 15 or 16 years old remembered me from working with him in 2001 in 1st grade. They all remember me.

I got started in the volunteer grandparent program because I heard about it and applied for it.

For a long time I had Mrs. Hamilton's 4th graders. One year I had 5th graders. I never liked geometry, but when I got in with the 5th graders, I learned something before the boys did, and those boys that never want to learn from a grandma, were happy I could teach them that. .

I mostly had three kindergarten classes each year. I always had five classes every day.

Being in a wheel chair isn't any problem for teaching kids. Being deaf or something is a problem. I was the only one of the grandmas who could run out and run races with them. Kids like to have someone play with them.

Being a volunteer grandparent is the best job in the world!

I think teaching kids for 18 years is the most fun I have ever had.

One of my students told me once, "My dad makes home brew." I said my dad made home brew too. And she said, "You know my mamma. I want you to meet my daddy." One time she was going home and she said, "You and Grandma are the only ones who have ever understood me." And she was correct. She made that drawing, and look, you can tell it's an old woman and a child. It's hearts and flowers, and that's what Richard (mother's computer friend), says I am. I think that's a terrific 10 year old child.

If I win the Publisher's Clearing House Sweepstakes I will pay to be able to volunteer! It's so much better than staying home and working contests. I miss the kids! They miss me and I want to work!

For my eightieth birthday the school had sheet cake and every child ate birthday cake with me! They'd never done that before.

This year the children at Shepard had a 'card shower' for my birthday. They got confused, and I received many that said 'Happy Birthday for my 90th birthday'--my goodness, it's my 83rd!

BIRTHDAY WISHES and More...

HAPPY 80TH BIRTHDAY

GRANDMA JANET !

Samples of the many cards and notes received.

Dear Grandma Janet,
You helped me so much with reading in kindergarten. I always looked forward to reading with you! I hope you have a happy birthday!   Sincerely, Grace

Dear Grandma Janet
thank you for all you do at Shepard. Your friend, Parker

Dear Grandma Janet, Thank you for monitoring at Shepard. It was a big help.
From, Hanna Weber, 4th Grade

Have a Happy Birthday
I hope you have the best birthday ever! From Tanner

There is no telling how much education these children have received just by observing Janet's usefulness. Relating to her, and seeing how a disability can be put to good volunteer use for someone else. The kids miss her. They want to know what happened.   *Where is Grandma Janet?*
Clara Sprague, Volunteer Grandma, Shepard Elementary

She's amazing. Most people under her circumstances wouldn't do what she's done. They'd crawl in a hole. She volunteers at school in a wheel chair.   Annette, Front Desk Mgr. Timbercreek

Thank you for the piece on Grandma Janet — Janet Barnes; it was a very nice article. Over the years, I've seen her around town and waited on her when she was a customer at the store I used to work in, and I always admired her tenacity and the way she just kept going.   It always seemed like she had a lot of guts, and I wish her a happy birthday coming up.   Anonymous

Janet started volunteering for the Foster Grandparent Program in September, 1997. She tutored children in the Columbia public schools and has been a positive role model for determination and self-discipline. One time I remember visiting her at Freedom House. We went outside to see her garden of tomatoes and green peppers in flower pots. She knew so much about many subjects

We talked about her "kids" and the impact she made on their lives. She often said," One of the reasons they keep talking to me is that we are looking eye to eye when we work together and they like that." Also, there was a boy that was in a wheelchair for a broken leg. She helped him adjust to his injury.

I enjoy Janet's quick mind and the knowledge and wisdom she has developed over the years. Her life has been full and rich. She serves others and by those actions enriches lives wherever she "Wheels."

Ann Gilchrist, Columbia MO
Foster Grandparent Director
Central Missouri Community Action

I have had the privilege of knowing and befriending one of the most beautiful women God has ever created. Her name is Janet Barnes. Janet is a "true beauty", because her beauty is both--on the outside and the inside. You can't spend long with her before her positive attitude, never-give-up spirit, and genuine love for others is rubbing off on you.

Janet has been a role model to me. I have watched her endure really difficult situations, yet she presses through, she never quits, never gives up, and always perseveres. She reaches out to others, and finds ways to bless them. I have admired her bravery and courage, and often asked myself, "If I switched places with her, could I even come close to walking through life with the achievements she has managed and the positive attitude she has maintained."

It has been such an honor for Janet to call me friend these many years. Janet – I sincerely thank you for taking the time to befriend me, model for me and love me.

Many blessings to you always, Becky Block

I met Janet Barnes one spring at the 9th Street Community Garden. The gardeners were working to get the garden ready for spring planting, and suddenly this little woman in a wheelchair came wheeling down the sidewalk and fearlessly entered the weedy path into the garden. The path was lumpy and muddy, and I was wondering if her chair would get stuck, but it didn't seem to worry Janet at all. This was my first introduction to a lady who doesn't let obstacles keep her from doing what she wants to do and going where she wants to go. Since that first summer, Janet and I have planted several gardens together, and we've spent many an afternoon talking along the way.

I can remember days when I was tired and drained after work, and feeling sorry for myself as I yanked weeds in the hot afternoon sun. And there was Janet talking about jokes her "kids" told her at school, or remembering someone who made her happy years ago. She has a wonderful memory, and has shared many interesting stories from her past, and things she has read about --all kinds of subjects. She could have complained about aches and pains or politics or life in general--but that's not Janet. She doesn't believe in wasting precious time worrying about what might have been, or how unfair life might be. It's just not her way to see the negative. Janet is a special person, and I am so fortunate to know her.

Sarah Lawson

As a young college student, I remember seeing Janet driving down the streets of Columbia over 20 years ago. Having been born with Muscular Dystrophy, it was inspiring to see someone happily aging with a disability. Through the years I've had the pleasure to get to know Janet, and to witness her impact on the community, and to personally be affected by her charisma and wisdom. She also reminds me to take care of my body, and eat healthier! Best of luck with your book, what an honor!

Aimee Wehmeier, Executive Director
Services for Independent Living
Columbia, MO 65201

I'd guess it was around spring 1987 that I met Janet. I was hanging out with my dog, somewhere in the middle of town, reading, trying to get away from folks, when she was rolling by, said hi, and we just started talking, or should I say, I just started listening. I've been listening to her now for almost 25 years. When I lived in Columbia, I'd eat dinner with her one or two times a month. We'd catch up on the latest, but mostly she'd shower me with her positive talk about her life, her philosophy, her crazy doctors, and so on. She is such an impressive person.

It's hard to sum up just how special Janet is. When I think of mentors in my life, she is at the top of the list. Rather than let her physical challenges push her behind the curtain, she has starred in so many people's lives including mine. I'm so honored and fortunate to have met Janet, and to have her as a friend and life teacher. I look forward to our continued friendship and more valuable lessons from her for years to come.

I know your Mom likes Haikus. I tried to come up with one for her last night. Here's a second shot at it.

Easy fade to grey
Against all odds blossoms bright
Flower among weeds

Thank you Janet!
Alan Polonsky Denver, CO

Betty Bogner, Sister-in-Law

I met Janet when she was about nineteen. Harold and she used to go from St. Louis, MO to Mt. Vernon, IL in a motor scooter with a side-car. She was on crutches and he was in a wheelchair. She would walk a little with a cane occasionally. She had to have many operations--feet, hand, arms...

She was a very strong woman. She had four children--loved babies. She held them all the time. She was always holding a baby.

She loved people. She was very intelligent. When I met her she was doing retouching for a photo studio.

I'm not as good at looking back as she is. I'm 78 and I've known her since I was 15 or 16.

She's had challenges all her life. She's done everything, and she can remember everything. She can go back to where she first met you and tell you everything, and it's correct.

Her mother (my grandmother and Betty's mother-in-law) was so good to her. She went above and beyond what a mother was expected to do.   When Janet had nervous breakdowns, she took care of you kids. I loved her.

Betty (Strong) Bognar,

What I Remember About Your Mom and Dad

How easy-going they were and how I never felt stereotyped by them because of my personality or weight.

How they were always curious to try things out. Such as the time I was visiting with you and they were in the kitchen eating rattlesnake and offered us some. Which led me to tell my father-in-law about them, after he had told me a story, about a young man he knew in his youth that tricked his parents into eating rattlesnake one time.

How strong they were. Others may have seen them as invalids. I saw them as normal people because they thought of themselves as normal people and acted as such. They were inspirational with their "have we ever tried that?" attitude. I have never known anyone before or since that had the same restrictions imposed by their bodies, yet went anywhere they wanted because they could drive themselves there.

Although you may disagree with me, I thought that they raised a great bunch of kids! (Even though I did have some serious questions about the oldest sibling at times!)

The trust that they placed in you and your siblings--it was amazing. I don't have kids, but I have managed to act like an adult/parent a few times and their actions have influenced me in ways I never really thought about until now.

I hope that my few contributions helped a little. I only got to be with the two of them a few minutes at a time, but every time was memorable because of their kindness.

(David) Matt Schmitt

Part of our lives during my high school years.

Angela Barnes, Daughter--Me

Life with mother and daddy was busy, interesting and productive. We kids learned that "bored" didn't exist. If we thought we were bored--we'd be weeding the strawberry patch or raking leaves, or...

Everyone had something to do. Daddy would be remodeling--I'd carry tools up and down the ladder to him. Mother would instruct me on how to make egg custard pie. We had commodity products, but she'd tell me how to make it and we had great food! There was never lack of activity--going to Our Lady of the Snows, ice skating, swimming with mother and daddy at Wohl Community Pool or camping, or...or...

My brother Gene threw a high-top boot at me once and I ducked. It broke the large picture window in the front. It was horrible and expensive, and for years I thought I was in trouble for ducking! Brian once pulled the electric coffee pot off the table while in his walker and got really burned. Robyn, while trying to peek at Christmas gifts early one year, heard mother or daddy coming and in jumping down, ripped and slit her thigh open on daddy's new BBQ grill with rotisserie.

We often had company. Birthday parties--mine in September-- were often in the basement, due to tornado warnings. We always seemed to include others in our celebrations and activities. Mother and daddy had friends--close ones. I saw many of them die young- -one, a young woman who went to high school with mother when I was around ten maybe. It was my first funeral and first open coffin. It upset me and daddy said "no more" for me to see. Young men and women died young, probably largely due to their own disabilities. My parents just kept working and doing--us kids, too.

Mother and daddy had a concrete sidewalk poured at church so they could get in. We all went to parochial grade school.

Paul Collins, Uncle

"SHE HAS THE RIGHT TO BE ANY DAMN WAY SHE WANTS TO BE. SHE'S EARNED THAT PRIVILEGE!"

P: (Paul) At one time one of Janet's ambitions was to play a xylophone. *(and she did)*

Your mother, without doubt had the first training wheels that was ever on a bicycle, at least where we lived. Guarantee Cycle made the wheels.

We always enjoyed each other. Just for instance, I don't know how old I was whenever they lived on North 11th Street, but at that time Ralph (mother's dad) had an old Hupmobile car. They quit making them a long time ago. We would sit in that car, and I would act like I was driving, and Janet would tell me where we were going to go, and I would imagine driving, shifting gears, making a left or right turn. We would spend hours doing that. It was just one of our little ways of enjoying each other.

When she and Harold got married, the same preacher that had married me, married them. At that time I had a '37 Dodge panel truck, I guess that's what they call SUV's now, but this was a panel truck, and I also had the back seat of a car sitting sideways in this panel truck. So in order for them to get married, I had a five-gallon bucket in the back of the truck, and also a bunch of tin cans tied on a rope laying up in the truck. We drove up to the preacher's house and he came out and he sat on the bucket to perform the ceremony, and after the ceremony was over, I just dumped all the tin cans and the bucket on the street in front of his house. He kind of wanted to scold me and said he didn't need all that mess on the street. I told the preacher, 'Don't worry about it." So when I drove off I was dragging all that. That's what people did for weddings. So that was how they got married.

A: (**Angela**) I know about them going out on the scooter with a side-car.

P: The wheelchair would fold up on the back of the side-car, and they'd put their crutches in between the side-car and the scooter, and they'd go off to Mt. Vernon.

I wanted that scooter so bad when they got rid of it. It was a Cushman, but I never got it. I guess at that time it might have been the only brand made, but it was a dandy.

P: I think they were going to go into the pet care business.

A: They raised dogs--Bassets and Chihuahuas--even tea cup ones.

P: In fact I started to pour concrete forms to pour a concrete sink at one time.

A: They ended up with concrete cages, faucets and pens in the yard. Mother and daddy made more money on breeding dogs and selling dogs than they made on their other income. So when daddy died, mother lost not only the social security they both had, but also the dog income. It was pretty dire for a while.

P: I didn't know that they had gone that far. Before they were going into dog business, they had a dog named Julie. Evidently they were having a bad time financially. Janet told me this story. They had been talking about a shortage of food, and Julie (dog) got out and got into the neighborhood trash cans, and brought the garbage back to them. That was just a pet, and that was a great dog.

Jill McClintock, Independent Living Specialist

I have had the privilege of working with Janet for almost five years. I have told her numerous times she is my role model, and she replies, "I deserve that," and she does. I have a disability myself and have struggled often with dealing with it, in particular the challenges as I get older. I asked her to contribute to an article on aging with a disability. I have struggled with pain, fatigue, and other issues. When I asked her what the secret was to successfully aging she replied, "I don't feel old--my muscles aren't what is best about me. What is best is my active brain." As I tried to get her to discuss the challenges of getting older, she continued to remain optimistic and stressed how she enjoyed living. In other words, she was telling me to get over myself and stop being so darn negative! I feel like she is my life coach, providing me lessons on how not to dwell on the negative, appreciate your "many blessings", "can't" is a bad word--determination is key, doctors don't know anything, and the sixth sense is common sense.

"I wouldn't trade places with anyone. I've done everything," she says. She has been a wife, mother, foster grandparent. Despite increased pain and challenges, she continues to stay active, tooling all around town even in the rain. She often visits me at the office, often with baby coupons and magazines she continues to receive in the mail even though she has made it clear she is 82! She knows I have a two year old nephew who benefits from this error. She also remembers my birthday every year and brings me a treat.

I have often said that should she write a book, I would be the first in line to buy it. What a remarkable woman!

Services for Independent Living, Columbia, MO

We have nine grandchildren.
Harold lived to see four.

Twelve great-grandchildren
that I know of... now more

CARDS BY JANET

Thank You!

Thank You!

Thank You!

A Saying,

The Greatest Gift One Can Give

Is of Their Time.

Thank You for Giving

   of Yours

I am appreciative,

Janet Barnes

A VALENTINE FOR YOU!!!

IT'S IN LOVING, NOT BEING LOVED
THAT WE'RE SUPREMELY BLESSED

IT'S IN SERVING, NOT BEING SERVED,
THAT LIFE TURNS OUT BEST

IT'S IN GIVING, NOT RECEIVING
THAT WE LEARN HOW TO GIVE.

IT'S IN LIVING YEARS OF LOVING
THAT WE LEARN HOW TO LIVE.

LIFE IS A MIRACLE AND THE RIGHT TO LIVE
IT IS A GIFT. IT IS WRAPPED IN RIBBON
AND WOVEN WITH DREAMS, AND
WHETHER YOU ARE VERY, VERY YOUNG,
OR VERY VERY OLD
LIFE IS FILLED WITH SUPRISES.

I FEEL PRIVILEDGED THERE IS A YOU
TO GIVE THIS VALENTINE TO!!!

By Janet--one of my best

THERE REALLY WAS A ST. VALENTINE.
HE LIVED 17 CENTURIES AGO. HE CONTINUES TO LIVE IN
US EACH TIME WE LET SOMEONE KNOW THAT
WE CARE ENOUGH TO MAKE THEM HAPPY.
I THINK EVERY DAY SHOULD BE
VALENTINE'S DAY!!! DON'T YOU?

*(The front is a picture of mother in a pink and red sweatshirt
with hearts and a great big smile...)*

ONE OF THESE DAYS I'LL BE FREE
TO DO EVERYTHING THAT PLEASES ME!

I'LL EAT PEANUTS WITH A SPOON
OR LIE DOWN TO REST AT HALF PAST NOON

I'LL CALL MY CHILDREN ON THE PHONE
AND ASK THEM FOR A PERSONAL LOAN

I'LL GET IN MY WHEELCHAIR WITH NO PLACE TO GO AND
INSTEAD OF FAST, I'LL DRIVE SLOW

I'LL KEEP MY LIFE SIMPLE AND
LEARN NOT TO FRET

I'LL TOSS OUT OLD PAPERS
I USED TO COLLECT

I'LL SMILE AT MYSELF WHEN I LOOK IN THE GLASS
AND SAY,
"HEY CUTIE, YOU'VE REALLY GOT CLASS!"

I'LL WEAR MY BEST CLOTHES
THE ONES I'VE BEEN SAVING

AND I'LL EAT ALL THE CANDY I'VE
SO LONG BEEN CRAVING

I'LL BAKE SOME FRESH COOKIES INSTEAD OF A DINNER
AND WON'T GIVE A DARN IF I DON'T GET THINNER!

I WON'T CARE IF I'M FIT, FANCY OR FAT
THERE WON'T BE TIME TO WORRY ABOUT THAT

AND SOON ALL MY FRIENDS WILL EASILY SEE
THE BRAND NEW PERSON WHO HAS ALWAYS BEEN ME!

BUT DON'T BE SUPRISED IF IT TAKES ME SOME TIME
I CAN'T DO IT YET. I'M STILL IN MY PRIME!

BE HAPPY

By Elizabeth Lucas, Revised by Janet

FOR ME CHRISTMAS, EASTER AND
THANKSGIVING ARE ALWAYS SPECIAL

HAPPINESS SHOULD BE TOO

TO BE HAPPY REQUIRES ONLY
A CHANGE OF YOUR ATTITUDE
IF YOU CAN'T CHANGE YOUR MIND
ARE YOU SURE YOU HAVE ONE?
IF YOU DON'T HAVE WHAT YOU WANT
WHAT DO YOU HAVE?

MERRY CHRISTMAS

(Picture of decorated Christmas tree)

HAPPY NEW YEAR

*(Back cover--picture of mother with Santa
and again a great big smile)*

When I was young, I wrote: A sequel to Joyce Kilmer's "Trees". It was about a place called home. It was the prettiest as one could please. I can't remember a thing about it, but it impressed me at the time. The poem was long, just couldn't quit. I do remember that it did rhyme. I don't how to write a poem in prose. I guess I could read, and think, and learn. Of all the poems that I choose, rhyming ones are the best. That is my unqualified opinion, of course. Each opinion expressed is our very own. Another may think to rhyme is the worst. I prefer rhyming for a poem.

June 7, 1994 Janet Barnes

Sequel to Trees

I know that I have always known
people more lovely than a poem.
Mature adults with shining eyes
complete enough to realize
when knowledge, we all do receive
surely everyone will believe.
A savior was provided, true
to walk his path is up to you.
This means to live as he did live
to love each one and to forgive.
Purpose wrong doing should not be.
Caring, helping, you'll see like me
the most wrong of which I'm aware
is hurting others, live with care.
Calm peace is like heaven to me
the good feel peace eternally.

The National Library of Poetry VIP #P0877308-066 April 28, 1997
"Wonderful verse! Select for the 'Sound of Poetry"

Together

Alone is a word I like never

Us is a concept of two together

One, when half of two beyond compare

Happiness alone is very rare

Things may fill the empty space

Companionship they do not replace

March 1995

Constructive clutter is better than idle neatness.

(To be read to apartment inspectors)

My Life in Haiku

Japanese poetry expressed in short stories
1st line 5, 2nd line 7, 3rd line 5

INJURY AT BIRTH
I'VE LIVED A CONSTRUCTIVE LIFE
DETERMINATION

COULD NOT STAND ALONE
INVENTED BIKE TRAINING WHEELS
RODE BIKE EASILY

PHOTO RETOUCHER
A GREAT JOB MOST OF MY LIFE
MADE PEOPLE PRETTY

LOVED BY A GOOD MAN
MARRIED, RAISED A FAMILY
WHAT MORE CAN ONE DO

PORTRAITS ARE VALUED
THEY LAST LONGER THAN PEOPLE
MOST SPECIAL TREASURE

ONE BABY MUCH FUN
TWO MADE TWICE AS MUCH PLEASURE
THREE, THEN FOUR, NOW WORK

PHYSICALLY I'M OLD
MY SPIRIT'S A SENSITIVE CHILD
EMOTIONS, YOUR GUESS

MOST IMPORTANT WANT KNOWLEDGE
AND UNDERSTANDING
ALL ANYONE NEEDS

WHY LIFE, ANYTHNG
THE CHILD IN ME QUESTIONED
ATTAIN PERFECTION

BEAUTY WHEN ALL THROUGH
WILL FOREVER BE IN YOU
IF SURFACE, COULD LEAVE

GOD PROVIDES THROUGH US
PLEASED WITH JOSHUA STORY
WE MUST BE DOERS

THE COLD REQUIRES WARMTH
THE HUNGRY NEEDS ENOUGH FOOD
TEMPLES MUST HAVE CARE

LACK OF NUTRITION
CAN CAUSE EXCESSIVE CRAVINGS
AND IMPULSE ACTIONS

IF THE VALUE'S THERE
IT'S WORTH WORKING, WAITING FOR
PATIENCE IS REQUIRED

WHEN TOTALLY STUCK
THERE IS NO BETTER SPOT TO BE
A WAY WILL BE FOUND

BELIEVE IN YOURSELF
KNOW YOU CAN DO IT, YOU CAN
TO SUCCEED, BELIEVE

DON'T BE SCARED TO DREAM
REALITY STARTS WITH DREAM
REALITY COSTS

I RESPECT ACTIONS
NOT PEOPLE'S TITLES OR RANK
RESPECT NOT EARNED HURTS

IF YOU'RE REALLY LOVED
YOU WILL FOREVER BE LOVED
IF NOT LOVED, YOU WEREN'T

LOVE, WHEN IT IS PROVED
NEED NOT BE DEMONSTRATED
NOT PROVED, WORTH NOTHING

BYE, A SCARY WORD
MEANS RELATIONSHIP ENDED
NEVER SAY GOOD BYE

IF IT'S GOOD. IT'S GOOD
IF NOT GOOD. NOT GOOD
DESTRUCTION NOT GOOD

SOME THINK WORRY'S WRONG
IT'S A GOOD MEDITATION
RESOLVED IT MUST BE

SHEPHERDS WERE WORRIED
OR THEY WOULD NOT LOOK FOR LOST
SHEEP MUST HAVE A LEADER

IF IT'S YOUR BEST
YOUR BEST, OF COURSE IS ENOUGH
NOT BEST. NOT ENOUGH

WHEN A CHILD, DAD SAID
SAY NOTHING UNLESS IT'S NICE
CHILDREN MUST BE QUIET

WHEN GROWN, SHRINE SIGN SAID
IF DOING IS WRONG, SAY SO
OR YOU ARE WRONG TOO

THE TURTLE'S NECK'S OUT
BEFORE HE CAN GET AHEAD
IT COULD GET CUT OFF

OBSTACLES ARE FOR
CLIMBING OVER AND TO GROW
THEN LOSS IS A GAIN

HAPPY LIFE IS WHEN
CONSTRUCTIVE RULES ARE OBEYED
OTHERWISE CHAOS

These are based on fact and opinion by Janet Barnes

My maternal grandmother, Mom Collins, asked Dr. Modert if the baby needed turned, and he went and took a nap. He didn't tell anybody I was a breach birth.

When he pulled me out, he broke my neck. She did ask him if I needed turned, because she thought I did.

She asked him "DOES THIS BABY NEED TURNED?"

He just gave my folks back five dollars for breaking my neck.

Your daddy turned puppies--the Bassets, not the Chihuahuas, because you couldn't turn them. We never had one born with a broken neck."

Personal Information

Mother: Janet Ernestine (Strong) Barnes
Oct. 9, 1928 - Sep.9.2013
Born Mt. Vernon, IL. Moved to St. Louis, MO 1939 and re-relocated Columbia, MO 1982
Best friend: Betty McFarland (lost contact after high school and searched for her all of her life)

Married: Harold Eugene Barnes, Jan. 1, 1949 (not leap year!)
Jan. 23, 1924-May 16, 1979

Parents:

Ralph Strong, Jan. 6, 1909 - 1978
Mary May Collins, Sep. 1, 1911 - 2001

Brothers:

Donald Ralph Strong, Aug. 17, 1930 - 1966
Stewart Edward Strong, Aug 28, 1936 - 1991

Children:

Janet Angela Mary Barnes, Sep. 25, 1949
Robyn Lynn Barnes, Oct. 9, 1951
Harold Eugene Barnes Jr., (Gene) Jan.12, 1954 - April 19, 2013
Brian Michael Barnes, June 17, 1955

Grandchildren:

Angela's daughters, Kimberly and Tiffany Barnes
Robyn's children, Jennifer and Christopher Goslin
Gene's children, Matthew, Crystal and Brandy Barnes
Brian's daughters, Amy and Tammy Barnes

Great-grandchildren: We have nine grandchildren. Harold lived to see four grandchildren. Twelve great-grandchildren that I know of. *(more now)*

Uncles:

Collins boys--they took real good care of me.

Ernst Edwards, called June, was shot in the stomach, and died when I was fourteen. The hospital let him die.

Paul Harold was my playmate.

Ervin Walter was tall.

John Henry spiced the beans too hot for anyone to eat.

Grandparents;

(Mom Collins) Grandma Collins (Mother's mother) was Henrietta Sara Jane. Mom's husband (Dad Collins) renamed her Jenny after a race horse.

(Dad Collins) Ernst Edward Collins

Mom Strong (Dad's Mother) her maiden name was, Maude Manchel and she was little, like my great grandmother Wilmore; great grandmother: Grandma Wilmore (mom Collins' Mother) came from Germany when she was eighteen. Her name was Evelyne Wilmore. Before she married her name was Karsh. She weighed about 78-pounds and was about 4 feet 8 inches. She had

a bakery and bought mother a bicycle and paid her to deliver her baked goods. She liked beer real good.

Five Generations:

Grandpa Wilmore, Grandma Wilmore, mom Collins, Mary Strong, and me (Janet) at 4-1/2 months.

On September 9, 2013, one month before her 85th birthday, Janet Ernestine (Strong) Barnes transitioned into the next phase of life. She now rests in the eternal love of God with her beloved Harold.

Do It Again, Grandma!

Thinking of Grandma & remembering being about 5 years old
& flying down College Ave. with Tiffany (sister) & Marsi (pet).

> The flags go down
> Grinning and pumped, gripping and straining
> Flying down the avenue, three to a seat
> Overtaking all, breaking the curve
> Shrieking and jumping
> "Hold on now girls"
> The red light flashes
> The wind dies down
> Wait..."Do it again, Grandma"

Not sure if you want to include that or not, it was a good memory
of Grandma. Cadence borrowed from Cake song, "Going the
Distance", but the words are mine.

Hope all is well. Love, Kim

Epilogue
(aka how the book was started and finished)

August 28, 2011 (Day 1 of writing the book)

 I did a lot of reflection on mother's book. I need to do some more. I need to actually type it out, so that the mistakes I can fix when I see her.

I thought I was writing the ending, but before the ending comes the part that tells the construction of the book.

So, after a number of mother's vignettes, and some of the comments of others, and the testimony that validates--no, that's not right. It is already validated--already authenticated. What these words do, is acknowledge and demonstrate in action to her, in ways that she can have and hold, that her life was experienced, lived, recognized, noted , perhaps completed. In my words "she got the job done."

The construction is once again done in my manner. What you're getting is what I have available, and what I can handle. What I could get were some of mother's words from her mouth, and transfer them verbatim to this paper you're seeing now, or to the words you may be hearing. What I have are comments, tributes, acknowledgements from others who have witnessed her life.

What you have is me, doing the best I can, to give you what I have available, and fleshing it with the benefit of having been present with her life at many different times to know it, and the maturity now, I hope, to offer it authentically to you without taint, or laden with emotion, resentment, confusion, blame or shame.

I think I accomplished what I started out to do!

October 27, 2011 (Book completion)

Book Two: MORE

Celebrate the Legacy

Mother's Letters, Writings and Thoughts
(unedited)

"Expressing feelings de-intensifies the feelings."

"What happens in me, is totally more important than what happens to me." Janet Barnes

Attitude

Attitude is more important than facts, beliefs, education, money, circumstances, failure, success, what other people say, think or do.

Experience develops attitude. Without experience we would have no way of having a healthy attitude. Altitude, the level one reaches is more dependent on attitude than aptitude, one's degree of education. Guess attitude really constructs one's belief system. Experience is important in building a good education and a healthy attitude. I will take what I get and make the best of it. If I don't have what I want, I will want what I have.   All you ever have to do to be happy is *change your attitude*. You can't always change the way anyone else thinks, but with determination you can change your own thoughts. Think constructively, let every experience be a developing process. No one should ever want to change the past. The past is a learning lesson. Be grateful, learn all you can. Work at remembering. For me there's nothing more important than memory--it gives reason for the past, acceptance of the present, and a belief in a better tomorrow.

What happens *in me*, is totally more important than what happens *to me*.

Attitude is the mind's paint brush. It can color any situation the way we choose to see it. I will find good in everything, I can't stand waste, I will find enough good in each situation, learn and grow so that what I've lived through is a benefit, not a disappointment.

Letter of Apology and Taking Responsibility

Dear Angela, Dennis and Girls,   October 15, 1979

The stuff came yesterday. Thank you. I've gotten well enough that all the things I bought while with you are of no importance to me now.

Angela, I wish you had kept those flowered shoes, they're pretty, but too big for me. I wish the girls had the owl and clown pictures too. I phoned before your birthday and asked Dennis to have you keep the cups for your birthday.

I'm going through your daddy's things. I wish you were here to take whatever you wanted. This is not easy.

I'm embarrassed at all the crazy things I did while with you. I would rather not have been around you and the kids while I was sick.

I thank you all for being so good to me, and so patient with me. Angela, it really upsets me--you being mad at me. Like I told Dennis, I wouldn't purposely do anything to alienate either of you. Both the boys left me after daddy died, and now you have left me too. Angela, you were better to me while I was with you than you have ever been. I really don't know what I've done to make you mad at that time.

There was so many things to be taken care of here. I've got the roof fixed so the snow won't ruin the upstairs ceilings this winter. Gene worked on it.

I'm not wanting to accept responsibility yet, but I have to. I need to find a buyer for his stamp collection, for Goose Creek (camp site), and I guess the acreage.

Angela, losing your daddy was enough for me to have to take. I'm not mad at anyone--please don't stay mad at me.

Mother

Computer Programmer Certificate

To: Dr. Wilson   June 9, 1984

When Dick Goodwin sent me to you, I told him I'd get a certificate if I could. All the people he sent to you before had not been able to complete the course. I felt this was bad on his record. Such a lot of taxpayers' money wasted.

The word impossible was not in my husband's vocabulary. I try to be just like him, so it isn't in mine. He said, "When it's considered impossible, that means it might just take a little while."

I got a certificate for Dick. Had written on back of my report paper, it does not say for the severely disabled. That would have really upset me.

I was placed in the advanced class. I finished the two-year course in one year. I completed to perfection 20 Cobalt programs. Told you I was a pretty good programmer when we parted. I did your school proud.

I am so grateful that Doctor Means granted me the opportunity to prove that I had not been too old to learn--grateful too for all the knowledge introduced that had not been taught at Todkomp.   I had never made poor grades before. My own self esteem needed to see if failing was caused by me or circumstances. My thank-you note to Mr. Johnson said, "This year makes last year's effort not totally in vain."

I do, not for merit or reward, what I do. I do because I have the ability to do it. I sure was pleased getting top grade among a class that was one that the teachers refer to as the best Columbia has to offer.

Greatest Compliment

My life didn't start at the time of one of my greatest compliments, but this and earlier tributes have been expressed because I have lived my kind of life. This happening took place a little over seven years ago. One of my seven granddaughters was eleven. She was impressed with me. She thought all kids needed the influence of a grandmother. Sitting, eating with me, worrying about her mother, I suppose she was thinking the problems she was having with her mother might have been because her mother had never met her mother's grandmother.

This child asked me, "Will mamma make it to heaven?" I said, "Yes, eventually everyone will grow up to be mature adults." She asked, "If you were eighty-four and hadn't seen me yet, you'd find a way to get to me, wouldn't you?" I said, "Yes." She then asked, "You wouldn't be the person you are if you weren't handicapped, would you?" I answered, "No." She said, "Whatever happened to you is exactly what needed to happen to you, 'cause I wouldn't change a thing about you."

Needless to say, she made my day and contributed in making my life. I wouldn't change a thing about me either. I'm not as important to her now as I was then and that's o.k.

Around that time we were both concerned about what would happen to her dad if her stepmother died. Her stepmother thought she was going to die. We were talking about this. She looked at me, and said, "I don't know what I'll do when you're gone." I told her, "I'm not going anywhere." For in those years I was her most important person. I took no chances. Crossed streets at stop signs, even if I had to go a block out of my way. Watched my nutrition even better than now. I meant it, I would be here for her. My need to be needed has always been my strongest feeling.

One time I had enough. This couple, my boy and daughter-in-law would call me collect, and ask me to do secretarial stuff for them. I never liked being a secretary. I was for my husband, but that was different. I called, took care of what they had asked for. I was fussing. Fussing is a good outlet for tension. I called back, and apologized for fussing, explaining they took care of my need to be needed, adding I THOUGHT MY NEED TO BE NEEDED HAD BEEN FULFILLED.

January, 1994

Writing Assignment--Graduation

As always, I've waited until the last minute to write my assignment. I think it was due two weeks ago. I said then I'd write on graduations. Mine was a little different, week-day--8th grade, mother and my youngest brother came by city bus.

It was June, 1942. There was a war. We dressed in white pleated skirts, navy jackets, and white blouses. It was raining when mother and brother went home. They had to walk a block. Mother's dress was egg shell, a new blend of crepe. It was really into shrinking. By the time she arrived home the bottom of it was up to her waist.

Stewart was five. He was embarrassed. So was mother.

At our high school graduation, I wore white taffeta. One of the girls in school was a cousin to Mayor Kaufman. He came to this graduation. I want to tell you about my prom at this time. It was in the evening. I borrowed a pink formal from Juanita Parkinson. Barry Barnett took me. He put my hands into white gloves and gave me a pretty light blue scarf...

January 4, 1998

Medication--The Effects on Mind and Body

April 10, 1992

The medications I have been given has been Thorazine, Haldol and Navane. Thorazine is my choice. Haldol made my blood pressure very low and made me feel so uncomfortable I couldn't have lived under its influence.

Navane gave me feelings of hostility and the most weird thoughts I've ever had. I'm never depressed.

The first time I was given Thorazine it wasn't known yet, but I was 4 weeks pregnant with my 4th child. Our boys were 17 months apart. My body couldn't handle this. I would not let my body give in until I collapsed mentally. I call what I do, taking a mental escape.

I was also given seven shock treatments between my 4th and 7th week of conception causing our son a learning problem. Instead of depressed I become elated. It was decided years later I had a hormone imbalance and now it is called a biochemical imbalance. I think it's my balance. I had no trouble after change of life, 1980 (my husband died the same year) until 1986. A doctor had found a nodule on my thyroid May 1984. It stopped my thyroid from functioning. September 1985: the medication became excessive causing my pituitary to stop. I had a lot of happenings in 1986. One was a para-psychological experience I wouldn't have missed for anything. I wouldn't have missed any of my experiences because I've learned from all of them.

When I get enough exercise, (which isn't easy since I can't walk), I don't have an acute biochemical imbalance. I ride an exercycle when I can, and this helps a lot.

I'm not assertive with my family because I've never been permitted to be. When I have taken more than I can take, feeling inhibited on my conscious level, I go to the next level. Probably the one Jung would have called personal unconscious where I'm not inhibited. We know it is normal to fight or flee when under too much pressure. I'm too little to fight, not physically able to flee. I feel no anger, so I've never been violent. I have suppressed libido tensions. I get drunk on emotions.

Once I called a man I had loved for 42 years and told him I had always loved him. He sent me a poinsettia, first gift in 41-1/2 years and I was overwhelmed.

The last two emotional drunk episodes were 11 months apart. Sometimes even longer than that. I'm taking one 25 mg of Thorazine each evening--my daughter's idea. My doctor has never given maintenance medication before. He has given me up to six Thorazine tablets a day when I behaved irrationally. He is writing prescriptions for this maintenance experiment. I'm willing to try it, to see if it defers me using my channel of escape. My daughter was having me take two Thorazines at night. This was too much. My doctor reduced it to one. This fits what happens to me when I take my mental escapes. It's a quote from Carl Gustave Jung, "When the shadow and ego work in close harmony, the person feels full of life and vigor. The ego channels instead of obstructing the forces emanating from the instincts.

"Consciousness is expanded and there is a liveliness and vitality to mental activity, not only mental activity: the person is also physically more alive. It is not surprising, therefore, that creative people appear to be filled with animal spirits, so much so in some cases the more mundane people regard them to be freaks. There is some truth to the relationship between genius and madness. The shadow (I add, Freud calls it id) of the very creative person may overwhelm his ego from time to time, causing the person to appear temporarily insane".

I am comparatively creative. If I'm to have a record here I would like this page put in it.

Angela asked me to prepare this statement for Barnes Hospital.   Janet Barnes

Letter to My Dad

August 4, 1992

The most authentic book I've ever read *Mind Probe Hypnosis* by Irene Hicks said we pick our parents where we can best learn what we are wanting or needing to learn to reach our highest potential. If that constitutes our interest, it must have been of interest to me to develop in as many areas as possible. You two were the best anyone could have come up with for this purpose. It didn't work with the boys. So for me to learn all I wanted to learn, I needed to be physically challenged. Not being able to get in or out of bed or off a couch, chair or car seat gave me a lot of time to think. I never thought destructive thoughts. Thinking was enlightening.

The two rules you gave me when I was eight were rigid but good. "A boy can ask, and a girl can say no" and "if you can't say something nice about someone you can say nothing at all." You didn't spank me much but the few times you did certainly caused me to be an obedient child and adult. I did tell on you (said something not nice) when you jerked my phone out of the wall and knocked me down when I was sixteen, attempting to call the police when you were choking mother. I always add, she was doing wrong, but I didn't want you killing her. I told your mother, my grandmother, and she said to me, "Janet, be good to your dad, after all he will always have to take care of you." These words engraved in my mind probably did more than anything to grow me up strong and responsible. I really didn't resent them. I used them to grow.

In the last few years there has been all the talk about child neglect, and I was neglected. I've had a little resentment and I say if you have reason to be resentful and you aren't, you're stupid. I use tradeoffs. We didn't have any child molestation. We lived a lot more right than that.

I didn't have a lot of fun. You drank, and I'm not too fond of being around drinking people, but I probably wouldn't have chosen so wisely when picking my life partner if I hadn't had you for an example.

I remember two funny happenings. You standing in the kitchen frying eggs in the middle of the night in your long dark top coat with no pants on. Another time when Eva and Aunt Katherine were visiting us, you went to the basement and built a fire in the hot water heater. When you came upstairs, mother asked you "Did you build a fire in your good pants?" You said "No, I built the fire in the hot water heater."

Knowing what I know now, all you needed was some kind of tranquilizer to help handle your depression. Mother wouldn't even let you take 'Nervine'. She said having to take anything was an example of weakness

You were the hardest-working person and you were the most honest person. I found a new ruling several years ago on a big sign in front of 'Our Lady of the Snows', that overrides your ruling about saying anything bad about a person. It said, if you see someone doing something wrong and you don't try to stop them you are doing as wrong as they.

If I had known you had emphysema, there would have been oxygen in your house and you could have lived longer. I was told you choked to death. Maybe that was better than a long illness.

(Nervine: A nerve tonic, a medicine used to calm the nerves.)

Letter to My Mother

Requested by Kristen Hays - Clinical Social Worker - April 26, 1993

Months ago, as stated in the letter to my dad, my most authentic book, *Mind Probe Hypnosis* by Irene Hicks, says we pick our parents where we can develop the most. I guess as an unborn baby, I already knew I would learn best by reverse psychology.

I didn't like your expression of love to male images. I can't call them men, only a boy would behave as they behaved and some of them were too old to be considered boys. I didn't like the way you professed love for me but would leave me to wait for hours before getting me up from bed. I never liked your dad. We didn't know he was alive until I was eight. From newborn on I didn't think it was fair that he had run off with a younger girl, leaving your mother with five kids and no means of support. You didn't see anything wrong with this. You just said mom [Collins, my grandmother] was too fussy to live with. He was a mechanic with his own garage. He could have sent money. He thought that playing dead long enough so that mom [maternal grandmother] got $500.00 insurance, freed him of responsibility. I didn't think so.

I blamed him for all the things that you did, not becoming a lady. I blamed him for Paul's stealing things, you all didn't even have enough food to eat. It takes food for mental development to control selfish behavior. I blamed him for your other brothers' somewhat bizarre actions. John's probably the most. You kids were deprived and depraved, and it left all of you scarred. When he made his appearance when I was eight, he had been missing from your life for thirteen years. I wasn't enthused about him coming back. It was important to you and I'm pleased he did return. You had worried about him all my life--feeding and asking every homeless person that came into town if they had seen him. The evening he came you weren't even aware that you left me on a

111

bedside pot for three hours after my bowels had moved. I pulled a tooth while waiting.

You put a 'T' on Jane, your mother's name and named me Janet. You put 'ine' on Ernest, your dad's name and made my middle name Ernestine. I had trouble being proud of that name until I realized in one of my psychotic episodes it was also my favorite uncle's name. I was born a very serious person. In these later years of happenings since Dad Collins died [maternal grandfather] I feel that everything is being done in dead earnest. It took a long time, but you five finally did grow up and made mature adult people.

John still had much lack of trust. It was difficult keeping $175.00 hidden in the basement in coffee cans. It's good that Katy told him before he threw the cans away as she started to do. When I was nineteen, I remember standing in John's driveway with Dad Collins. I was wearing white long pants, red and white tee shirt. He had his arm around me. I told him people I care for, I feel compassion, not passion. He thought that unusual. This influence which I think is good, feeling compassion instead of passion, was probably attributed to his life. In my judgment he lived a life ruled by passion. His desires and wants had to be fulfilled no matter who it hurt. There's a page in *The Prophet* by Kahlil Gibran that states if you can learn from someone's mistakes, you should be grateful. I am and I commend them, not condemn them. So far as I'm concerned this Pisces, (symbolized by the fish) grandfather of mine is off the hook. I can't say "All's well that ends well." Too many people were hurt by his selfish behavior.

I really did blame Dad Collins [grandfather] for everything that happened. Maybe that's why I was always able to not ever be angry with anyone, no matter what they did. He was just a name you told me about. I didn't think he should have run off and play dead. Unique grandfather, granddaughter relationship.

Fantasies

June 26, 1995

A couple of years ago I was just about to fall asleep when the phone rang. I roused and answered it. Richard, my computer friend, who asked: "Do you ever fantasize?" I said, I don't think so." "He said, "I mean dream dreams when you're awake that can't come true?" Again I said: "I don't think so."

I told him of saying to Harold before we were married, "if I can have a child, I'd like to have a Libra daughter to grow up to do the things that I couldn't do." I meant, roller skate and such, not divorce and hurt husbands. We had two Libra daughters. Second one born at twelve noon in the middle of my birthday. That wasn't a daytime dream that couldn't come true.

When Robyn was born Harold was twenty seven, I told him "I'll give you a son for your thirtieth birthday." I missed it by eleven days so that wasn't a daytime dream that couldn't come true.

When we were kids, my brother had a great imagination or maybe he was fantasizing. He would run in from outside many times a day and tell us what worms had said to him and what he said to them.

The other day I was remembering thoughts of my childhood. I definitely did fantasize then when I was about eight because I remember telling my mother, "When I grow up I'm going to have fourteen kids and bring them to you and put them in your refrigerator." That was a daytime dream that did not--could not come true.

Story based on true fact by Janet Barnes

Fear

President Franklin Delano Roosevelt said, "There is nothing to fear, except fear itself." I totally respected this man but I don't understand his understanding of this quote. Maybe if I analyze this enough it might make sense. I always analyze everything. I tackle it to oblivion. I never went that deep into this statement.

One basic fear is being left alone longer than I can go without physical help. It could be a long time if I'm up in my chair. If I didn't go anywhere, my batteries would probably stay up three days. I couldn't handle being left alone nearly that long if I were left in bed. I get anxious if no one shows up when I'm in bed. When I get anxious my bowels get loose, and I feel like I have to go to the bathroom. I've reliably handled this but it isn't easy. I try always to have a back-up person or two. Having a back-up de-intensifies the degree of being anxious, thus makes waiting less difficult.

The provider responsible for getting me up, the one who did the scheduling repeatedly forgot to schedule me. Often she would tell me who was coming but forget to tell the person. I could be left alone a long time. All we could do was call an answering machine and hope someone would check it sometime. I never messed my bed, but I lived a miserable life. I feared more than fear. Guess my life wasn't in danger unless I died of embarrassment if I couldn't wait.

(name withheld by author) said it was all in my mind. About that time, one of my good, good attendants, Shelly, had a cat that never had any trouble waiting all night to go outside. One night the cat went in the kitchen cabinet under the sink, the door was closed and she was locked in. Her bowels moved all over the space in the cabinet. Shelly and I accepted this as proof that any variety of animals had real feelings of needing to go to the bathroom when trapped. It's a tangible animal response, attempting to free itself of an intolerable condition.

I haven't yet found any resolution to cause me to believe there's nothing to fear except fear itself. I'll keep working on it. I will also always have a back-up or sleep in my chair. I really have a fear of being trapped.   November 18, 1996

Letter in Support of Garden Coalition

May 2, 2005

I've been gardening for years with the Garden Coalition. I eat a lot of green leafy vegetables. When Tom Dudzig (not sure the way to spell his last name) was our helper, he thought I would never get enough green leafy vegetables. Not sure anyone can get too many.

I'm 76 years old, not on any prescription drugs. I take vitamins and I eat fresh food from my garden several months a year.

When Guy Clark was with the Coalition, we would taste different growing things, clover, even grass. I always grow tomatoes, peppers (bell and hot), dill, swiss chard, parsley, sage, and onions. Tomatoes are considered to be the best antioxidant a person can eat. I bring all my green tomatoes home at the end of the season. I ripen them as needed. I always have home grown tomatoes for Christmas, usually New Year's and one time January 6th.

Think the purpose of this letter or note is to encourage people to help sponsor our Garden Coalition. If I were in an income bracket high enough to owe taxes I would donate to the Garden Coalition. We help keep people healthy.

Sincerely

A Letter to Amy and Howard

June 11, 1994

Dear Amy and Howard,

I'm sending a copy of the 10 rules for a happy marriage. Author unknown. This has good guidelines, Guess, I've followed this line of thought. My life has been and is great. Congratulations, be happy. I won't be able to come to your wedding. I'm going to St. Louis for your daddy's birthday the next day. I won't have any way of coming to you. Real pleased I was able to be at your graduation.

10 Rules for a Happy Marriage

1. Never be angry at the same time.

2. Never yell at each other unless the house is on fire.

3. If one of you has to win an argument, let it be the other one.

4. If you have to criticize, do it lovingly.

5. Never bring up mistakes of the past.

6. Neglect the whole world rather than each other.

7. Never go to bed with an argument unsettled.

8. At least once every day try to say one kind or complimentary thing to your partner.

9. When you have done something wrong, be ready to admit it and ask for forgiveness.

10. It takes two to make a quarrel, and the one in the wrong is the one who does the most talking.

I Am the Most Fortunate of People

Dear Angela,   February 12, 1998

I'm the most fortunate of people. I have always believed I have enough disability to totally appreciate the ability I have. I would not trade places with anyone. I've been so privileged to find what I searched for, and I search for everything. The answers or knowledge is already in my head before the occasion of necessity is there. I am grateful for this.

Years ago I read, "We pick our parents so we can do what we want to do in this lifetime." I knew I picked right. I don't know if any other parents could've let me live a full, eventful life more capable and more productive than most able-bodied people. I never felt handicapped until after your daddy died and I was thrown into an able-bodied world where I didn't feel wanted. Harold and I could do anything and everything together, and did.

When you said I shouldn't have kids, I checked out my book again, this could be an answer to you thinking that. "One of the rare eager ones, who was so eager that she pushed others aside and rushed in, mistakenly getting in the wrong family." Another one when asked why she had chosen her family replied, "the body was available". Further questioning obtained the same response. When she heard her tape-recording she responded with, "Next time I'm going to be more discriminating."

Probably you remember when Mr. Via, a rehab counselor for your daddy tried to have you girls taken away from us. You were four. I don't think it disturbed Robin, she was two. It seemed to be hard on you. We were not forceful people. If it had been decided we weren't fit to be parents, we would've given you to whoever could do the job better. Mr. West, a psychologist, sat in the kitchen every Wednesday from eight till 12 for 6 weeks. His finding was that you two could not be in a better home.

Mr. Via hadn't been of any value as a rehab counselor. All he could think of was that daddy could be a bookkeeper. Daddy had been given a fourth grade tangible education at Missouri Baptist Hospital where he lived from age 5 to 22. He could make change as good as anyone, but he didn't have secure feelings about mathematics. He had no interest in bookkeeping. So no more Mr. Via and no more fear of losing you girls. Then we had Gene.

My wedding vow was to try and make up for all the pain and unhappiness your daddy had lived through, and to help him have all that any other man could have. This included a son. We had girls, a car and a home. I told him when Robin was born, when your daddy was 27, "I'll give you a boy for your 30th birthday". I missed it by 11 days. We didn't order Brian, he was a rhythm system baby. I told him that once, and I got back to him quickly to make him know that I didn't know what we would've ever done without him. He was with us through hiatal hernia hemorrhaging surgery and heart attacks. He (Brian) and I took the clothes for daddy to be buried in, picked the casket--we took care of the funeral and bought the tombstone.

By the time Brian married and left I had learned how to stop Harold's choking. The flip-flopper in his throat, like an automate choke in a car, would raise up from gas caused by excessive acid. When Harold slept soundly enough to snore, the liquid would go into his lungs instead of his stomach. At the first snore sound I would touch his shoulder and say: "Turn over Harold, you're snoring." He would turn to his side without waking, slept, and didn't choke to death. For years he had choked when eating. The first time his choking happened in bed, Brian was there before I called him. Harold was blue. Brian forced him into a sitting position and banged him back to life. I couldn't do all that so I had to learn a way to keep him alive. I have learned to do a lot of things that physically I really couldn't do. When it's for survival, you'll find a way.

I said to Harold before we were married, "If I can have a child, I'd like a Libra daughter to grow up and do the things I couldn't do." I meant roller skate and such. You were born Libra, Robin was born 12 noon in the middle of my 23rd birthday. You all were born early, eight-month babies. I'm responsible for any deficiency you may have. There's lots of development that last month. Would have carried you all longer if my body could have. Brian is the only one that was a completely premature incubator baby.

No idea what you wanted to do with your life. I wanted to be needed, and not hurt anyone. We never stopped you from doing anything.

Gene never called me anything. His kids call me and mother by our first names. Robin called me mother. Brian seemed content to have us for his parents. You've called me mother and you've been pretty good to me.

The Effects of Medication—Again !

Dear ...   April 9, 1995

I owe one of your drivers an apology, and if he had any medical expense, I'll pay it. I'm just now coming to. My daughter has had me on drugs and it's not fair to me or anyone for me not to be in the hospital when I'm doped. Today I remember running into a driver's legs about two weeks ago. I don't know which one. It was not premeditated and it isn't that I don't like him. I was living through flashbacks of when my brother died, when my mother beat me, giving me a black eye and bruising me so badly all over my arms that I was kept locked up so no one would see me for seventeen days. I feel no malice toward her. We all went a little crazy when my brother died. When she hurt me so bad, I pushed a chair into her legs.

I'm uni-polar manic. Not bipolar manic depressive. I normally become more enthusiastic and have more fun buying some match box cars. This time I bought toy motorcycles. I have never spent more than $36.00 on a spending spree. I took back $12.00 of that the next day. I've never bounced a check or used a charge card. My doctor says this is not very manic. I don't believe in any of the conventional outlets for tension--pain, illness, drinking alcohol, using drugs or living promiscuously, and I can't perform the acceptable outlets, walk, jog, dance, or swim. Crying is a good one. Could do that, but I won't. One man I know that is as physically limited as me, says he cusses as an outlet. So far I can't do that either. I do what I call "Flip my lid." I go to another level of consciousness where I am not inhibited. A couple weeks later my determined, inhibited ego takes over again and I'm a very pleasant, and responsible for a couple of years or more. I didn't last year. I waited till the anniversary of my brother's death. One of my doctors said he is going to teach me to cuss.

If any of you see me acting weird, call ... Tell them I'm a client of Heart of Missouri Mental Health. They will get me help and I'll be back good as new in two or three weeks.

When you're physically challenged and differently able, I mean really physically challenged and differently able, you are not a 'give me' person. You do everything you can for yourself and those you feel responsible for. It is hard for me to take, even though I know I'm as deserving as anyone.

I'm grateful for everything, even the difficult. We accepted responsibility like it was a God-given privilege. I didn't carry any of our children more than eight months. They might've made more mature adults if I could've carried them nine months. I study everything. I will learn from everything. I will find good in everything.

Harold and I worked well together. We had an eventful, never a dull minute life. We made concrete sidewalks, floored the basement, replaced lead, stopped up pipes with galvanized. Harold would read a book, put in a bathroom. He wasn't a quad. He had two good arms. He was a paraplegic. He'd read a book, wire the house. We paid the city inspectors $315.00 to inspect the wiring so we could get a new meter. Doing never stopped. We also did the best we knew how to care for our four kids, we gave them what they needed, and some of what they wanted.

When we started this endeavor there were no curb cutouts, no SSI, no accessible housing. We paid $4000.00 for a house before Angela was two; $400.00 down and $40.00 a month. Remodeled it, made it pretty. Outgrew it when Brian needed a baby bed instead of the bassinet. Traded it in on a $9,000.00 store building. We got $5,000.00 for our pretty little house. Made the store building pretty. Harold practically built it. Even put in a small pool in the backyard with a pulley and sling seat where he could get me in and out.

Harold lived long enough for me to get a widow's pension. It was decreased 18% for every month I was under 65. I was 50. My widows' pension was $50.00. Our Social Security had been $350.00. In 1975, our combined income was 175.00. I could've gotten SSI. (disability income) I didn't.

Some Proud Moments

June 3, 1997

(Discovered by author on Nov. 18 '14 12:56 a.m.)

I've had happy times--like when I was told I would graduate with my class from 8th grade after missing more than half of the year. My grades and my final tests were better than most of my classmates. One of them was almost 21, couldn't go another year. I was 13, so I could have been detained. Not really considering his grades and my grades I may have graduated by default.

I've had triumphant times that fulfilled my life. Our daughter and son-in-law left a two-month-old granddaughter that didn't have a functioning adrenal gland with us for two weeks while they went to Colorado to buy a house. The baby did not have a functioning adrenal gland. An injury could cause her to go into shock and die in ten minutes. We would have had to get her to a pediatric endocrinologist for a cortisone shot within ten minutes. I felt proud that they entrusted this child with us instead of Dennis' parents. I told Dennis this when they returned. He said, "We knew you could do as good with her as anyone."

My triumphant time was at my daughter Angela's birth. We had been told after x-rays that I couldn't give birth because I was too small and I had a bend in my pelvis. Dr. Roy Walther Jr. was a resident doctor. He had provided my prenatal care, had admitted me under his dad's name the day before she was scheduled for Dr. Anstee to take her by C-section.

At seven in the evening as Harold was leaving I started to hurt. He said, "You think we're going to get a baby?" This was new to me. I did know, if I couldn't give birth, I had to stay calm, try to prevent her from moving until Dr. Anstee could get to me, and the operating room which was in use could be available. My resident doctor, Harold's friend, lifted me into the bed with rails around it in the labor room. He would walk the halls and steps, look in on me every fifteen minutes. He was as worried as anyone could be. Couldn't locate Dr. Anstee on a Sunday evening. The operating room was still in use at 9:30 p.m. After laying there in the labor room two and a half hours motionless and silently hurting as bad as I've ever hurt. I heard Dr. Walther say after examining me, "Call up stairs and tell them I won't need the operating room now." He took me to the delivery room, lifted me again to the delivery table. He could see and reach Angela's head. Placed forceps in Angela's temples. Put me to sleep. She was born 10:10 p.m. Three hours and ten minutes of labor. This was as good a job as any woman could have done. Maybe for the first time in my life I felt equal to any able-bodied person.

The next morning when Dr. Walther came into my room, I asked, "Can I have more ?" not that I like hurting, but my vow to God when I married Harold was to try and make up for all the pain and unhappiness Harold had lived through and to help him have all that any other man could have. This included a son. Dr. Walther said, "That one got through, I guess the rest can."

Random Entries--Mother's Log

(unedited and unaltered--mother's actual typed words--one thumb key press at a time)

1997 THURS 17th SHARON 6:10 HEARTS AND FLOWERS JOG SUIT OATS. OATS TOOK ME TO ALUMNI CENTER FOR VOLUNTEER RECONITION BRUNCH

MAY 1997 =96 THURS 1st SHARON 6:14 RED PNTS WHITE BLOUSE RED FLOWER 298 EGG SALMON AND MAYONNAISE SANDWICH. CALLED ROBBIE, ASKED THAT THE DRIVER PICK ME UP AT P.O. WENT TO BANK, CASHED TAX RETURN CK. BOUGHT P.O. MONEY ORDER 100 DOLLAR. SENT EXPRESS MAIL 10.75. MIGHT GET TO TEXAS TOMORROW FOR SURE BY 3 SATURDAY. BUB TOOK ME TO WORK. LOT OF DELIVERIES.

MAILED JURY DUTY LETTER BACK TO COURT HOUSE. FOLKS CAME ABOUT 4:45. **BATTERY PACK TOO LOW TO GET ARROW ON THE VAN.** WAS GOING TO TAKE
THE RANGER, ANGELA RELEASED THE WHEEL HUBS TO BRING IT IN FOR ME TO TRANSFER. LEFT WHEEL WOULDN'T LOCK AGAIN.

1998 MON 12th SHARON CALLED TOO MUCH ICE. DEB GOT ME UP ORCHARD CRAB LEG SALID. **CHECKED PARKING LOT TO SEE IF ANY ATTENDANTS CAME, SLID TWIRLING AROUND, AND STOPPED IN THE MIDDLE OF THE STREET.** CAR SWIRVED OR I WOULD HAVE HIT HIM. RUSSEL SLID FEET FIRST AIMED FOR MY CHAIR SO I COULD STOP HIM. SO MUCH ICE, SO
SLICK WE COULDN'T GET ME BACK ON THE WALK. ASKED HIM TO CALL 911, HE SAID THAT'S FOR AN EMERGENCY. I SAID, THIS IS AN EMERGENCY. HE WENT IN TO GET TOM UP. A MAN CAME BY, HELPED
ME GET ON SIDE WALK. I WHEELED TO BUS STOP RAMP, COULD GET UP IT. HE PUT HIS COAT OVER ME, RUSSEL WENT FOR MY WRAP. SHARIFF CAME AND LEFT. 1 FOR THIS DISTRICT CAME. HE TOOK A BLANKET FROM HIS TRUNK, THE 2 MEN STOOD ON IT FOR TRACTION AND INCHED ME UP OVER NEXT DOOR GRASS. RUSSEL TOOK MY WRAP IN, ASKED IF
I ALMOST HAD A HEART ATTACK, TOLD HIM NO, TAKE THINGS CALMLY.

WATER IN BATTERY: MARATHON,3P **1-1-98**,MAGNUM **1-22**,RANGER **1-29**,NEW JEL BATTERIES IN MAGNUM 2-20, DENNY PUT NEW PLUG FOR RANGER JEL CHARGER ON MAGNUM **3-17**

BOOK TO READ: CELESTINE PROPHECY - AMASTAD, WHY THINGS CHANGE BY JEANNE BENDICK, THE LIFE GAME: EVOLUTION AND THE NEW BIOLOGY BY NIGEL CALDER, DEATH IS A FACT OF LIFE BY DAVID HENDRIN, THE FINAL MYSTERY BY STANLEY KLEIN, DEATH IS A NOUN BY JOHN LANGONE, ECOLOGY: SCIENCE OF SURVIVAL BY LAURENCE PRINGLE, THE TENTH GOOD THING ABOUT BARNEY BY JUDITHVIORST, LIFE AND DEATH BY HERBERT AND BLEEKER, SONIA ZIN. READ DEATH IS NATURAL BY LAURENCE PRINGLE, TALES OF A CHINESE

1999 ICE TONIGHT, SLEPT IN CHAIR AGAIN.kidney stones,

2001 NO ONE CAN BREAK ANY OF THE TEN COM-MANDMENTS WITHOUT RECOMPENSE, IT'S IS A NEAT WORD, IT MEANS PUNISHMENT AND REWARD. SO EVERY
ONE WILL RECEIVE RECOMPENSE. TOOK ME TO URGENT CARE. DR. JENNIFER JIANG PRESCRIBED "ULTRAM" PAIN PILL, DRY HEEVES AND CHILLS. FAXED PRESCRIPTION FOR HOYER TO HOME PATIENT ALSO GAVE ME PRESCRIPTION FOR PHYSICAL THERAPY

STAYED HOME, HURT BAD LAST NIGHT, UP TOO HIGH IN BED. HURT LEGS LOTS.

2003 SHERRY FORGOT ME, I CALLED HER. SHE
WAS UPSET, WOULDN'T SIGN PAPER. SHE PUT ME TO BED.

PHILIPS HAS SOME ANGRY KIDS. TOLD HER I FEEL ANGER IS A NON CONSTRUCTIVE ATTITUDE. THE ONLY ONE IT HURTS IS THE ONE WHO IS ANGRY. DOES
NOTHING TO THE ONE CAUSING ANGRY. THE WAY I HANDLE THIS, AND IT WORKS FOR ME. MIGHT CAUSE OTHERS TO BE ANGRY. THAT'S THEIR PROBLEM. EVERYONE IS DOING AS GOOD AS THEY CAN WITH WHAT THEY HAVE TO WORK WITH. NO ONE WOULD BE WRONG ON PURPOSE. WE LIVE ON DIFFERENT LEVELS OF KNOWLEDGE AND UNDERSTANDING. I KNOW

ANGER CAUSES HIGH BLOOD PRESSURE, HIGH BLOOD PRESSURE IS DETRIMENTAL TO YOUR HEALTH. I HAVE ENOUGH PROBLEMS WITH THE LIMITATIONS I WAS BORN WITH. I DO NOT NEED KIDNEY FAILURE OR HEART ATTACKS, ANGER MAY BE THE CONTRIBUTING FACTOR TO MOST OR EVEN ALL ILLNESSES. WITH THESE NEGATIVE FACTORS TO ANGER, I WILL DEFINITELY CONTINUE TO SEE THE OTHER PERSONS VIEW POINT AND FEEL ENOUGH EMPATHY AND COMPASSION TO NEVER BE GUILTY OF HAVING LACK OF CONTROL THAT COULD CAUSE ME TO BE ANGRY. LIMITATIONS CONTRIBUTE TO BEING THOUGHTFUL OF OTHERS. THUS, FOR ME LIMITATIONS HAVE BEEN BENEICIAL. MY GRANDMOTHER TAUGHT ME, WASTE NOT, WANT NOT. I APPLY THIS LESSON, NOT JUST TO FOOD, OR MONEY. IF I'M HURT, DISAPPOINTED OR STOLEN FROM, I WILL SEARCH UNTIL I FIND SOME GOOD, THEN IT'S NOT A WASTED EXPERIENCE. I'VE EXERCISED MY BRAIN, MADE THIS BE BENEFICIAL

JANUARY 2004

THURS 1st VICKI 5 ORCHARD JOG PNTS GRAY SW SH ORCH PNK CAKE & COOL WHIP FOR OUR 55 WEDDING ANNIVERSARY. COLD STAYED HOME. PORK SANDWICH, SALAD FOR LUNCH. TAPED & WATCHED SOAPS.M

DREAMED **1-22-04** Dreamed about animals. I looked up, saw big animals on electric wires and telephone poles. Bears, Lions and Tigers. The one that stood out was a Leopard above and Tommy right. Later when I thought again about this dream I was influenced that Leopards really can change their spots. There was a long coat beautiful cat, dark shade of blonde. Real pretty name, don't remember. It was representing me and the name meant everything good and beautiful. Pretty dream.

5-7-04 NEW BATTERIES IN QUICKY

FRI 2nd VICKI 5 GREEN JOG PNTS WH POINSETTIA SW SHIRT. OATS BANANA. I STAYED HOME, WATCHED SOAPS.

SAT 3rd VICKI 5 GREEN JOG SUIT GOLD PEACE ON SW SH DONUT BANANA. 2 EQUATES 12:30 AM. WOKE BRIAN 7. BOWELS MOVED 8 & 8:30. GOOD. SOUP AND SALAD

FOR LUNCH. MARIBETH CAME AT 3. TOOK ME OFF POTTY
CHAIR, PUT COAT ON ME. I WENT TO MASS.

TUES 17th VICKI 5 TEAL JOG PNTS NEW PNK SW SH TEAL
FLW SANDWICH SOUR CREAM. WOKE BRIAN 7. CAME FOR
CK FOR KILGORES.MATT CAME FOR ME 8:30.

THREE BUSSES WERE IN FRONT OF SCHOOL. WE WENT TO
THE BACK, NO PLACE TO PARK, I SUGGESTED ATT NOSE
IN OUT OF THE WAY TOWARD TRAILOR, SCHOOL,
DUMSTERS. GOT OUT, WENT TO THE CURB PARALEL WITH
SIDE OF SCHOOL. ORANGE CONES WERE ABOUT A WALKS
LENGTH FROM THE CURB. THAT WAS WHY WE HAD NO PLACE
BY A WALK TO PARK. WE HAVE TO HAVE A WALK TO SIT
THE LIFT DOWN ON. A GOOD SIZE WHITE BOX BED TRUCK
WAS PARKED OUT SIDE OF THE ORANGE CONES IN THE
CURVED DRIVING AREA. I HEADED BETWEEN THE CURB AND
CONES TOWARD THE CURB CUT OUT, SOMETHING
ATTATCHED IT'S SELF TO ME. STARTLED ME, I SAW THAT
TRUCK THAT HAD BEEN PARKED IN THE DRIVE AREA. WHEN
I LOOKED TO SEE WHAT WAS DRAGGING ME, I SAW TOE
WHITE SIDE OF THE BOXED IN BED OF THAT TRUCK
PULLING MY WHEEL CHAIR. ALL I COULD DO WAS BE
DRAGGED ALONG UNTIL I COULD GET TO THE CURB CUT
OUT. WHEN I FORCRD MY CHAIR TO TURN INTO THE CUT
OUT, **MY LEFT FRONT WHEEL WAS CAUGHT BY THE LEFT
CORNER OF THE CURB, DUMPED ME OVER WITH QUITE A
JOLT. BENT LEFT FRONT CASTER WHEEL UP UNDER
THE SEAT OF MY CHAIR AND I HIT THE GROUND WITH
THE IMPACT OF THE 280 LB. CHAIR PUSHING ME.** I HIT
HARD. PEOPLE WERE THERE QUICKLY, MATT & SOMEONE
PICKED ME UP, PUT ME IN MY CHAIR. IT
WAS NARROWER. THEN IT WAS SAID, THAT I PROBABLY
SHOULD NOT HAVE BEEN MOVED. MRS. WEAVER WAS THERE,
DONNA.

SOMEONE SAID THE POLICE DIDN'T WANT TO COME
BECAUSE THE ACCIDENT WAS ON SCHOOL PROPERTY. I
WANTED A POLICE REPORT. SOON I SAW MEN IN UNIFORM.
I THINK THEY WERE POLICE. AMBULANCE CAME, TOOK ME
TO MISSOURI UNIIVERSITY HOSP, DONNA WENT WITH ME.
HAD A COMPLETE EXAMINATION NEW SWEAT SHIRT CUT
OFF, BROKE SAFTY LOCK ON MY DIAMOND CUT ROPE
CHAIN. AN UNCOMFORTABLE NECK SUPPORT LEFT ON FOR
HOURS AND INTERVENIOUS LEFT IN.

CALLED BRIAN, AFTER I COULD TELL HIM I KNEW I WAS OK. HE WAS REAL UPSET. AFTER HE SAW MY CHAIR HE CAME RIGHT OVER TO SEE THAT I WAS OK. KEPT SAYING, GOD WAS WITH YOU. TOLD HIM, I HAVEN'T DONE ANYTHING FOR HIM NOT TO BE. I HAD ASKED MATT TO TAKE BROKEN CHAIR TO SEATING & POSITIONING. BRIAN SAID MATT HAD BROUGHT THE CHAIR TO MY HALL.

DIDN'T GET LUNCH UNTIL 4 PM. ATE MY HAMBERGER FLAT ON MY BACK. CALLED VICKI, BROUGHT MAGNUM WHEEL CHAIR AND CLOTHES. I CALLED MRS. WEAVER, SHE SAID WE COULD UNLOAD AT WHEEL CHAIR PARKING IN FRONT. CALLED DOTTIE, SHE HAD BEEN CRYING, SAID I COULD HAVE 5 HRS. TOLD HER I HAVE WORKED SO HARD THIS YEAR TO COMPENSATE FOR THE 2 HOURS I LOST LAST YEAR, OFTEN I'M TOO TIRED TO BREATH.

MY NURSE, VINCENT TOLD ME AT 8:30, YOU CAN GO HOME NOW. CALLED VICKI AT 9, CAME FOR ME WHEN THE BALL GAME WAS OVER. (prov had 9 h 50 m acc) (VICKI signed for 3 hrs today + the 9-10 that made 3 h for her help)

MADE CHILLI MAC, PUT RAMON NOODLES IN MY CHILI.
FEB 21st 2004

MY STOMACH HURT, I WANTED TO LAY DOWN, DIDN'T HAVE THIS PROBLEM IN TILT BACK RANGER. WAS LAID DOWN AT 10, WENT TO SLEEP, MY STOMACH QUIT HURTING.

FRI 27th VICKI 5 HOT PNK JOG PNTS WH BLOUSE PNK FLOWERS 1/2 PBJ CRACKER BANANA. WOKE BRIAN 7. RICHARD CAME 9 ISH. WAS GOING TO PAY HIM 30 FOR 32 MORE MB OF MEMORY, THE MEMORY HE BROUGHT DIDN'T WORK IN MY PACKARD BELL. HE BROUGHT 100 SPEED NEEDS 66 SPEED. WE WALKED TO COMPUTER PLACE ON WALNUT, HE HAD CALLED THEM, AND THEY DIDN'T HAVE WHAT WE NEEDED. MY MAGNUM WENT WILD AGAIN. RICHARD HAD TO HOLD THE CONTROL NOB WHILE I UN-LOCKED MY DOOR. I STALLED IT IN THE BATHROOM, TURNED IT OFF, IT STARTED O.K. THIS TIME. I CALLED UNITED, RICK WILL SEND STEVE TO SEE ABOUT INVACARE. RICHARD THINKS HE HAS PRINTER SET WHERE IT WON'T LOCK UP. ATE TUNA CASSEROLE, SALAD, BAKED POTATO WITH LOTS OF BUTTER.

ROB HAD GIVEN MATT THE MESSAGE TO CALL ME. MATT CALLED AT 3:44. THE OFFICER HAD TOLD MATT THE TRUCK HIT ME. MATT TOLD HIM HE DIDN'T SEE THE TRUCK HIT ME. I CALLED MATT'S ANS MCH EVENING, **TOLD IT MATT COULDN'T HAVE SEEN THE TRUCK HIT ME. HE PULLED BESIDE ME, HOOKED ON TO ME, PULLED & DRUG ME. WHEN I LOOKED TO SEE WHAT WAS PULLING ME, THE WHITE BOXED IN TRUCK BED WAS CLOSE TO THE LEFT SIDE OF MY FACE.** WHEN I REACHED THE CURB CUT OUT I JERKED FREE OF THE TRUCK. MY LITTLE LEFT FRONT WHEEL CAUGHT ON THE LEFT CORNER OF THE CURB CUT OUT.
THE TRUCK JERKED ME OVER, THE FORCE OF A 260 POUND CHAIR MAKING IMPACT LANDING EVEN MORE EXTREME. I DIDN'T LOOSE CONSCIOUSNESS.

JAN 2005 VIC TOOK ME OFF POTTY CHAIR AT 2. (pca-15m) I WENT TO 4:30 MASS. DIDN'T GO TO THE SUPPER. CAME HOME I WAS COLD. CALLED ANGELA, TOLD HER MY PHONE HAD BEEN OFF. SHE HAD TRIED TO CALL.

WED 2nd VICKI 5-6:15 GREEN JOG PNTS YELLOW FLOWERED SW SHIRT CHILI WEENERS CRACKERS. DWIGHT 9 & 2. QUIANNA & I WROTE ABOUT HOLDING THE BABY. JAYDA & SKYLER READ TO ME. SEVERAL OF MRS. FRETWELL'S KIDS READ TO ME, BRIANNA READ BEST, NOT FAST & MEMORIZED. KALEB WAS VERY ASSERTIVE, HE TAUGHT ME A LOT, HE TOLD ME HE HATED ME. I READ TO JOSIA, HE HUGGED ME. VALERY GAVE ME NOTE, I LOVE YOU. BAKED POTATO FOR LUNCH. WENT TO LIBRARY WITH MRS SICTS KIDS, THEY WERE ALL SITTING UP. CAME HOME, IT WAS PRETTY WARM, ABOUT 60, RAN TO MY BANK WITHDRW ANNUITY.

JANUARY 2007 MON 1st, TUES 2nd, WED 3rd, FRI 26th VICKI 5 GREEN JOG PNTS GOLD SWEAT SHIRT SALID SANDWICH. NO SCHOOL, ANGELA CAME, WE ATE FIRST, WENT TO DR. MEHR. MY HIMOGLOBIN WAS 11 LAST MONTH, WOMEN SHOULD HAVE 12, I WANT 14 LIKE I ALWAYS HAD. HAD BLOOD WORK. WENT TO BANK, GAVE MONEY TO ANGELA. WENT TO WALMART.

FEBRUARY 2007 THURS 1st, RRI 2nd VICKI 5 GRAY JOG PNTS PINK SWEATER STEW MAYONAISE BREAD. SCHOOL. STARTED ANTIBIOTICS.

MON 5th VICKI 5 GRAY JOG PNTS PINK SWEAT SHIRT GRAY CATS SANDWICH SOUR CREAM. STARTED ANTIBIOTICS FROM DR. MEHR LAST WEEK, NOT WELL AT ALL.

THURS 15th VICKI 5 GRAY JOG PNTS PINK SWEAT SHIRT GRAY CATS CREAM OF WHEAT. CALLED OATS & SCHOOL, ALLERGIC REACTION TO ANTIBIOTICIS. I AM BEING DROWNED & CHOCKING.

FRI 9th VICKI 5-6:30 PINK JOG PNTS PINK SWEAT SHIRT GRAY CATS CHEESE SANDWICH. VERN TOOK ME TO FSTER GRANDPARENTS FOR A MEETING. THEY SERVED CHEESE, CRACKERS & PASTERY. GOT STUCK IN BATHROOM, CALLED 911. LEARNED THE ONLY WAY TO GET FREE OF 911 IS TO TURN PHONE OFF.

MON 12th VICKI 5-6:15 DEEP BLUE JOG PNTS MAROON SW SHIRT BLUE TRIM HOT DOG SOUR CREAM MASHED POTATOES. RAY TOOK ME TO SCHOOL 9, HOME 2. IN MRS. GOULD'S ROOM 30 MIN WHILE SHE GAVE INSTRUCTIONS ABOUT A MATH GAME. TRENTON CAME OUT WITH ME, DID THE GAME, FILLED OUT A PAGE. I TOLD MR. ROBINSON I LEARNED WHY I DON'T PLAY GAMES, IT'S EASIER FOR ME TO DO IT ALL IN MY HEAD THAN MOVE THE CARDS. I HAVE EXCILLERATED THOUGHT PROSSES & INTENSE FEELING I WOULDN'T TRADE FOR PHYSICALLY ABILITY. TRISTON WROTE ABOUT SUN & MOON, COMPARISONS. HELPED KEAJAUNEE. LISTENED IN MRS. HAGERS.DEN.

ABOUT SUN & MOON, COMPARISONS. HELPED KEAJAUNEE. LISTENED IN MRS. HAGERS.DEN.

Haven't I had the most interesting life
you've ever heard of?

Janet Barnes

MORE:

Comments, Tributes, Prayers Kept Coming

Services for Independent Living

Independent Living Center of Mid-Missouri, Inc.
1401 Hathman Place
Columbia, Missouri 65201
800-766-1968
573-874-1646
(TTY) 573-874-4121

There are certain people that come into our lives that impact your life in a profoundly positive way. Janet was one of those people. When I first met her, I was still living at home with my parents and trying to live up to the title of Independent Living Specialist. I wanted to do everything right and lacked confidence and quite frankly was still trying to accept who I was as a person with a disability and the challenges that come with it. Yes, I offered support and guidance to Janet, but she returned the favor. Every time I talked to her or saw her, I knew she was going to impart some lesson or words of wisdom that I could benefit from. Janet really changed one's perspective on life. She taught me the physical challenges do not define who you are. Your mind, attitude, heart, and spirit are what matter. Even when your body is weak and in pain, you keep on persevering and living life to the fullest.

I am so grateful for the many hours I spent with Janet. She made a profound impact on me the minute I met her. I always told her she was my role model which she felt was richly deserved. While her body was frail, her spirit and determination were strong. She had a beautiful and generous heart and I am a better person for having known her.

Lessons from Janet:

1. Do what you can to prove the naysayers wrong
2. Stop complaining
3. If I can do it so can you
4. Doctors don't always know what they are taking about
5. Live your life to the fullest
6. Don't waste food. Mind your manners
7. Become a foster grandparent
8. Take pride in your accomplishments
9. Share your wisdom with others
10. Fight for your independence

Thank you Janet for sharing your wisdom and life experiences with me. You were a great teacher.

Jill

Jill McClintock
Independent Living Specialist
Services for Independent Living

MAXIMIZING INDEPENDENCE FOR PEOPLE WITH DISABILITIES

I have known Janet for a long time. I was her caregiver for a few years and we became friends. I would see her at Sam's Club or Walmart and have a great visit with her. She babysat my daughter one summer for a few weeks. She is our role model.

Lana Carter

I have known Janet for 27 years. I worked for VNA when I first met her. She is a very busy lady and has given us good advice on a number of occasions.   Alice Van Dyke

After seeing Janet traveling by wheelchair in the snow and ice, I felt the need to meet her. I introduced myself to her outside of Walmart last fall. I explained how much I admired her. She told me, "Don't admire me, and never feel sorry for me; I get around better than most people with legs." She told me her stories of being an aid/teacher in the schools, and spoke sweetly of her daughter and son. She told me she didn't take many pills and explained how bad they were for her "little body." She went on to explain the chemistry behind her healthy condition.
Carla 05/09/2012

I know Janet personally and this book is a great tribute to her life. We should all be inspired and maybe ashamed of what we haven't accomplished as able bodied people. Janet let nothing stop her --she is so amazing. This book needs to be used as reading material for newly handicapped people for therapy to show them they can do whatever they want.   Shauna 07/31/2012

I first met Janet in 1984 or '85 when I was finishing my undergraduate degree in Social Work at MU. As an intern for the Division of Aging, I got to work with Janet. She was living at Freedom House. Janet was a challenge to me in that she was so independent and self-assured that I was not sure what I was supposed to do. Many years later, I would see Grandma Janet cruising the halls of local schools and assisting children with special one-on-one learning. I feel very sure that so many students, like me, learned far more than they expected from Janet. Her presence and generous determination and resilience expanded our views of the capabilities of all human beings.

I remember Grandma Janet from elementary school...she was always my favorite school Grandma. To this day I always see Grandma Janet on her busy travels to and from school and I always wave! I am soon to graduate from the University of Missouri and believe that Grandma Janet has played an influential role in my life and the life of many others.

Molly Williams 04/25/2012

Mother's will to live and her courage to do this with obstacles, pain, and overwhelming odds motivated me to actually complete my first '21-day complaint-free diet'. This is something I have aspired to do since October 2006 when I first learned of this concept.

I've made headway--some times better than other times. I even once went quite a few days in a row. Some of the time I was alone, but even alone I could dwell on criticism or complaints in my head.

This time, with her accident I made it. Sometimes I just had to not comment and refrain from a conversation, but I MADE IT.

I believe in every cell that mother has raised the bar on what qualifies as a complaint. Even now--today--July 6th 2012 while sensations and feelings are returning and pain is present, she smiles and does not complain.

I haven't continued as well, but seeing and knowing her makes me a much more conscious person, and more than not an easier person to be around.   Angela Barnes

I am stunned. I just saw her three weeks ago cutting through Stephen`s Lake park in the rain, I felt bad the car I was in was not equipped to give her a ride. The woman is unstoppable. As long as she still breathes I will not lose faith in her fighting spirit.

Les Masters 04/24/2012

Grandma Janet used to read to me at Shepard Boulevard Elementary School. I am a 19-year-old and moved to Springfield recently to go to college. Before I moved here I worked at Hy-Vee on Conley Road in Columbia. I used to see Grandma Janet in there all the time and I would have conversations with her about Shepard. I knew she didn't remember me, but she was such a kind lady.

My name is Sam from Kenya, in Africa. I have come to know so much about you through your daughter Angela. You've truly been an inspiration to many people who probably might never meet you in person, but you've greatly influenced their lives. I feel honored to know you.

I just finished your book, and I have to say I feel like I've known your mom forever and I have never even met her! She is an amazing woman. It really is an inspiring life she has led and is leading. It sure made me re-think the way I think. Through reading this I realized that we only have limitations if we let our minds wander in the direction of limitations. I don't want to limit myself anymore, because if I'm not sure I can do something, I'm going to give it a try and I may just surprise myself by being more able than I think I am.

Teresa Neville, Collinsville IL

Grandma Janet is such a wonderful and giving person. She read with my son when he was a little guy at Shepard, and even filled in as his "grandparent" one year on Grandparents Day at school.

Yvonne Lee 04/25/2012

I miss visiting with Janet and she's in my prayers. Tell her that Ellen says "Hi," and is looking forward to chili dog lunches again.

My heart, my prayers, and my tears go out to you and your family, Angela. I don't know you and your mom, but I read the story of her accident in 2012, shortly after I moved to Columbia, and started following on Face Book. I knew no one here. Reading her words and inspiration through your posts I knew that if she could challenge the odds, I could, too.   Julie Brown

Janet, I am very proud of the life you have made for yourself. You are one strong lady. I cannot fathom everything you have gone through and the things you still have in front of you. You are a woman to look up to.

Theresa Barnes, daughter-in-law May 8, 2012

She always said she wasted nothing and she always had an answer. She loved those kids at school. She would do everything she could by herself. She did ask for someone to open a door for her (if she had to). The kids were so disappointed. Where is Grandma Janet? She did a great job.

Clara Sprague, Volunteer Grandma Shepard Elementary

90-pound heavyweight, the story of the remarkable life of Janet Barnes, touched me deeply with its simple message of living life as well as you can. Janet's absolute refusal to allow any roadblock or challenge to stop her will inspire readers of all ages. She has lived a life of courage and love. Her daughter, Angela, has done a wonderful job of helping her mother tell that story.

Kate Martin, Editor, The Perryville Buzz, Perryville, MO

I was Janet's home health nurse for about 2 years. She is a feisty lady and I bet she will pull through! I hope she can overcome these obstacles! If anyone can she can!   Sheila, RN

Hello, my name is Brenda and I wanted to say, Janet, you are in our prayers. Whenever I would come to Columbia to shop or see friends I would see you out and about and would say to myself, "What an inspiration. We wish you the best recovery."

Heart of the Matter

People in the Pews:
Meet Janet Barnes

By Sophia Pingelton

"I have had an interesting life." That is the phrase smilingly quipped by Janet Barnes, and it certainly seemed apropos after talking to her recently. You may see Janet at any of the masses at Sacred Heart as well as about town.

Janet was born in Mt. Vernon, IL, and proudly celebrated her 80th birthday this year. She has been a foster grandparent to many children in Columbia over the past 15 years through the Columbia Public School system [Columbia, MO]. She assists the teachers at Shepard Elementary School with five classes (each consisting of as many as 22 children) in reading, writing, and arithmetic "and to attempt to turn out gentlemen and ladies." Janet added, "Wherever I go in all directions I hear 'Hi, Grandma Janet' from children around town. They are wonderful; they're just like my own grandkids." Speaking of grandchildren, Janet has nine grandchildren and 12 great-grandchildren from her own four children. She has two daughters, Angela of St. Louis, MO and Robyn of California; and two sons, Harold [Gene] of Mt. Vernon, IL and Brian who lives here in Columbia. "The girls came first, and I told my husband I was going to give him a son for his 30th birthday. Well, I did pretty good, I missed his birthday by only 11 days." laughed Janet.

Janet lived much of her adult life in St. Louis where she married her husband, Harold. Janet shared, "We got married in a panel truck. My husband used a wheelchair and I didn't think it was right that his bride would be standing and he wouldn't. My aunt and uncle were our witnesses, and the minister married us in the back of the truck, with all of us sitting on a panel." Janet and Harold later joined the Catholic Church in 1953 together.   Janet thoughtfully continued "Harold and I were inseparable. I made a vow to him that he might be able to have all any man could have and make up for any unhappiness he ever had." They were married for thirty years before Harold passed away in 1979.

While Janet worked up to 14 hours a day retouching photos at home for a St. Louis photographer, she also juggled raising her four children. Her husband "did the work of five people" working at Missouri Baptist Hospital in St. Louis before they married and later at Alexian Bros. Hospital. Janet worked retouching photos for 24 years.

After Harold passed away, in 1979, Janet decided to move to Columbia to learn computer programming. She finished a two-year program from the Career Center in one year at the top of her class with A plus grades. Janet enjoys doing graphic arts and designing greeting cards on her home computer.

Although she uses a wheelchair to get about, Janet's spirited attitude is an inspiration. She concluded, "I have never lived a handicapped life. My parents were told I wouldn't live past 14 because of an accident [born with a broken neck], and here I am. A man pulled his car over once and said "You motivate me, I see you everywhere doing everything.""

"I have always taken what I had and made the best of it." Indeed a wise sentiment of which we all need reminding occasionally. And *yes, Janet, you do most certainly have an interesting life.*

What an amazing woman! I have known her as a volunteer "Grandma" at Shepard school since my oldest, now 16, started kindergarten. Four of my five children got to know "Grandma Janet" during her many years at Shepard. She is an inspiration and blessing to so many. Our prayers will continue.   Kristin

Janet, we have met in the hospital, where you were are always delivering flowers and books to others, along with your heart-warming smile. We've also met in church although you are usually an 11:00 a.m. person and I am an 8:30 a.m. mass person. I have always been amazed at your strength and the confident way you went about your daily tasks, you have served others so joyously and well. Now take time for your own healing. Know that God holds you, and your church family holds you in their prayers. Let that wonderful spirit shine through and guide you to your return to health. Praying for you daily.   BJ Rodeman

Please tell your mom that she continues to inspire all who know her and those who learn about her, whether via this website, Facebook, or the 90-pound heavyweight book!   Gregory Hilbert

I was Janet's personal care attendant in her own home for a couple years and even continued to volunteer to take care of her after I lost her as my boss. I have followed her progress from one hospital to next, and have visited her almost daily. I have taken her flowers out of my garden and I always get a smile from her. She has a love for flowers and all living things and her eyes light up smelling my roses.

If she could talk right now, she'd be talking my head off, which I miss very much. She'd tell me daily she has more to learn, more to teach, and more to do, and I truly believe that for she is proving that yesterday, when I visited. She was very alert. Smiled at my flowers and smelled them, which lit up her eyes. I also moved her hands around a little, and touched the bottom of her left foot, which she responded by slightly moving her leg. That inspired me and I called her daughter, Angela. I put the phone to Janet's ear and she had different expressions as if she understood, and I believe she understands everything. I can't wait till she can talk

Tammy Kirkman 6/26/2012

Thank you!
Mrs. Weaver

You are an inspiration to us all. Carri

Thank you for being a role model for life-long learning.

Thanks for all your reading ♡ ing

Janet, Thanks! Ms. Phillips

The children so look forward to reading w you!

Thanks for giving your time so freely!

♡, Kathy

from your Sacred Heart friends

npgs happy birthday

Wishing you a comfortable day filled with pleasant thoughts to cheer you

Happy Mother's Day!
Rita Schultz

With love from all of us.
Peggy Bohnenkamp

We miss you Janet! Glad you are well!
Maria Cox

Hanni ♥ Jolly

June we miss you Janet I hope you feel better soon.

Jolly happy birthday

Janet
We all remember & miss your the hospital staff church. Happy Mother's Day! Sue & B.J. Rad Station

Happy Mother's Day Lester Kugle

BEST WISHES, MIKE SARRAZIN

Love and prayers, Cindy & Jim Chapman

140

The Human Factor

 Janet Barnes – the first time I heard the name is still clear in my mind. I was in the therapy gym at the hospital finishing up for the day when one of the other therapists asked, "Did you hear who's coming?"

I remember taking a deep sigh and asking, "Who?" Janet Barnes wasn't someone I'd previously worked with, but was someone who was, in her own right, a celebrity. After all, she had just been inducted in the Guinness World Records as the 'Longest Living Quadriplegic" (incomplete).

I was to evaluate her. I really wasn't sure what to expect. I read her chart. She had been living independently for a long while. She was a quadriplegic since birth. [Therefore] I began to discount her potential success before I met her. From my training and experience, you determine from the types of patients with similar medical histories whether they will be successful, or whether they do not have a great prognosis. The fact that she was a quadriplegic since birth presented me with a stigma on her ability to come off the ventilator and be successful.

Not only did Janet Barnes not fit the stereotype, but she was an exception. I learned the great lesson of not judging a book by its cover [or a patient by appearances and/or history]. I had a preconceived idea of potential outcomes due to my educational background and personal experiences.

After evaluating her, my expectations changed! Although she was on a ventilator and unable to communicate verbally, she was able to communicate with appropriate head nods as well as follow my directors. She was no stereotype.

In the beginning there was reluctance to allow her to take her variety of supplements added through her G-tube. There were concerns of possible drug interactions and our liability. However, one of our respected doctors said it best. "If she got to be 84 years old taking these supplements she's obviously doing something right."

This was a perfect example of looking at a patient as an individual allowing them to continue their way of life – even it did not match a protocol.

Over the next eight weeks our speech, respiratory, and pulmonary group worked together. We could see the suggested changes were making her stronger day by day. Janet continued to make slow and steady progress towards independence. It is so important that we, as a team, help make the appropriate suggestions for our patients, and thereby assist in their success.

Janet's next stop would be to a skilled nursing facility... She was to use that opportunity to continue to gain strength with the goal to transition to an acute rehab facility. My fear was that although a facility may take a tracheotomy patient, they may not have a staff that can adequately meet the needs, or identify if something was not right.

Before she left, I visited her on her last day at our facility. She looked great. Her headband was in place along with her smile. We hugged. I said, "I'm proud of you," and she replied, "I'm proud of you." We had helped one another in the eight weeks we spent together – the lessons she taught me will continue as I grow within my profession.

Continuing education is expensive and at times conflicts with our work hours. However, the payoff is priceless. Ultimately, it is our job as healthcare providers to want to do better. When we have patients we are unfamiliar with, it is our job to find out what we need to know to properly care for them. We can ask ourselves, "If this was my grandparent, would I be okay with the care I am giving?"

Janet Barnes will be missed. She touched many lives, and will forever remain in my memory. She reinforced the idiom, "You can't judge a book (or person) by its cover."

Celia Montes, Speech Therapist

Excerpts of an Interview with Janeen Erickson

A: How did you meet mother and how did she affect your life?

J: (Janeen) I met Janet when I was in nursing school. I had a couple of kids to raise. Janet, more than anybody had an amazing attitude – what others thought of as less than whole.

People who walk, or don't have any problems, react differently – she never complained, she found out about people, and she had a fantastic memory. I'm the same age as she, but can't remember my grandchildren's birthdays, but she did.

She was constantly searching for--like algebra you are not looking for an answer, but looking for a better question – she was always looking for the spiritual – she studied all the different ways – always wanting to understand everything.

She was open-minded and took it all in, and – she told me more than once that she wanted to live no matter what shape she was in--especially when discussing Christopher Reeves. She just had a very strong desire – that life is such a gift, even if she could not say anything or more – but she said her strength might inspire someone else.

She was not sure if we had more than one life, – but if so, wherever she is -- she is still helping others.

Rain or shine, snow or no matter, she went places.

She most inspired me by "just her"--her love of life, her choice not to let the circumstance of her life or her disabilities stop her. If there was a wheelchair marathon she might have done it.

Any time I start feeling sorry for myself, I think of Janet, and how silly it is to feel sorry.

She had reason to complain, but never did. She raised concerns about where she would like to see change, especially for other people – how she could facilitate a change for others – to change what was not fair.

Not everyone who is old or disabled wants to die – and they still want to get more out of life. Somebody can be in pain or some kind of distress, emotional or physical, and still want to be here. There are people, like Janet who felt that she had something to give or something to offer. It is a real shame to lose someone like that.

You cannot help but love her. Her last words to me were, "Never stop learning." She wanted to keep learning. She said, "The more you learn - you learn, not to be prejudiced, not to be ignorant, and to get the most out of this life that you could – learning about people – learning about everything."

When you first look at Janet, you might think "what a poor thing" – but when you get to know her, you change your thoughts. She was not shy.

I think she was aware of the ignorance around. She was pretty smart – she paid attention to everything that was going on.

I think there are other people out there like Janet, and who are making a real difference, but no one pays attention because it makes them uncomfortable.

We are cheating ourselves by not getting to know them.

A: Thank you Janeen. I am glad to know that her words and examples of her life will be used in teaching others to pay attention.

The Lights Went Out--Mother's Lights Stayed On

February 11, 2013

Conversation with Bev (wife of resident at nursing facility)

Last night we lost our power, and it was spooky because it just went "coop" (describing sound). The magnets that hold the doors open were all released and all the doors were slamming.

We were all concerned --our little vents didn't seem to have much power. The battery backup wasn't working right so we had a lot of things going down. The poor respiratory therapist (RT) kept running back and forth to give air with the bags (manually pump), to pump the air into the people on respirators.

Meanwhile with all these things going down, all were talking about Miss Janet's light being on. There was no power anywhere else but in Miss Janet's room.

It was kind of weird --we had no power. Only Miss Janet had a little lamp that stayed on. It was like all the angels were there with her keeping an eye on her. She looked real peaceful when I got to her and made her covers more comfortable. I told her how wonderful it was that God was looking out after her. She gave me a smile -- she looked so sweet and she closed her little eyes. She wasn't a bit worried.

We must have had about an hour there that we were having problems. We had a lot of people running back and forth. The certified nursing assistants (CNA's) were helping to manually pump. I just don't understand why the batteries didn't work. I'm a little worried about that.

A Few Medical Updates . . .

May 12, 2012 "Hey, this is Dr. Christ just talking about what we did in surgery today. We fixed her left hip socket with a screw and a small plate and we removed part of her external fixator around her left knee. We put in a plate to fix the top part of her shin bone, and then added some more pieces to her external fixator across her left ankle. We also plated her right tibia break that she has by the right ankle. And hopefully won't have to do anything with the little bone on the right side which is the fibulae bone. Potential surgeries on the horizon would be for her arms."

What it meant was mother broke nearly every bone in her body and somehow they were able to put her back together again...

August 7, 2012 "I think she has done remarkably well for her significant injuries and has done better than we all probably expected. She is having great stamina and recovering well for her significant, significant injuries. She's doing well."

Brett D. Christ, MD, FACS,
Associate Professor of Orthopedic Surgery, Columbia, MO

In answer to mother's question, "Am I mending?" Dr. Ricci stated, "She's all healed. No restrictions. Activities as tolerated."

Dr. Ricci, Barnes Hospital Chief of Orthopedic Surgery

(This was about three months after the horrible accident.)

"...for those of us who have inspired to have a career serving others in healthcare related activities, this tiny lady's should be studied carefully. In the interaction with our patients and their families we need to stop and take time to get to know them well. By doing this, we will be better providers, our patients will have better outcomes, and we will develop a better understanding of the importance of the human side of medicine."

John P. Lynch, M.D. Vice President and Chief Medical Officer, Barnes-Jewish Hospital, Professor of Medicine, Washington University School of Medicine.

"As I (Dr. Christ again) have been able to talk to Angela and review the book about her mother, Janet Barnes' determination and the way she lived her life undoubtedly played a role in her ability to survive the significant trauma she experienced on April 23, 2012 and during the time I took care of her.

She arrived to the University emergency room with multiple injuries after being struck by a motor vehicle while in her wheelchair. She sustained multiple injuries including fractures of both arms, multiple areas of her pelvis, both legs at multiple levels, and her 3rd lumbar vertebra. Once she was stabilized, she was transferred to the intensive care unit. Six different specialist teams were involved in managing her complex injuries during her time at University Hospital. She underwent 15 different procedures during her stay to address all of her injuries. I believe we were all amazed that she was eventually able to leave our facility almost one month after she arrived."

Mother's youngest memory...

"Will I be able to do enough to deserve the air I breathe?"

Her last concern...fear...

"Will they see me as defective and think it merciful to let me die?"

I make other instructions as follows: *kept alive at all cost. I do not want my parts used by any one but me.*

Janet E. Barnes

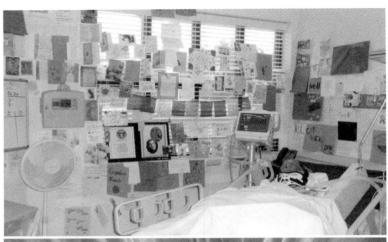

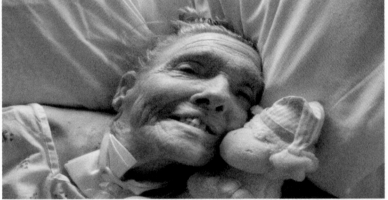

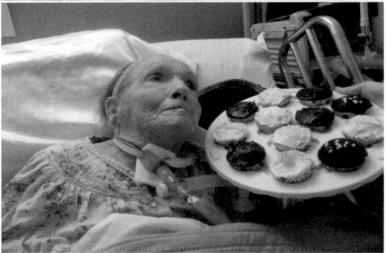

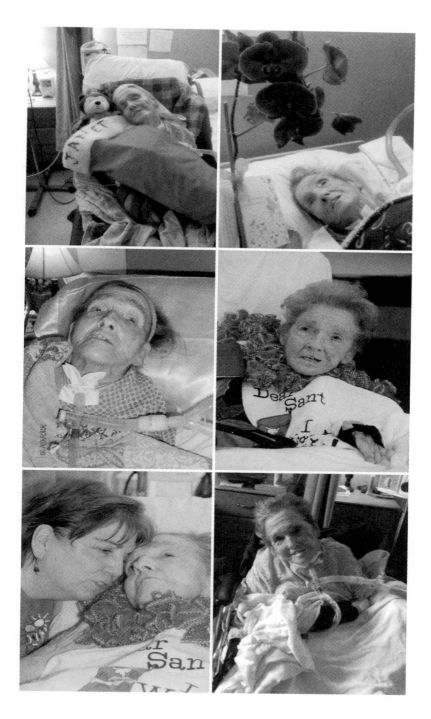

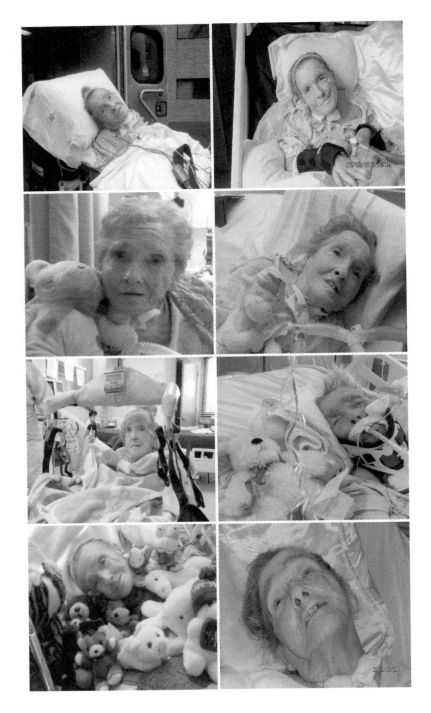

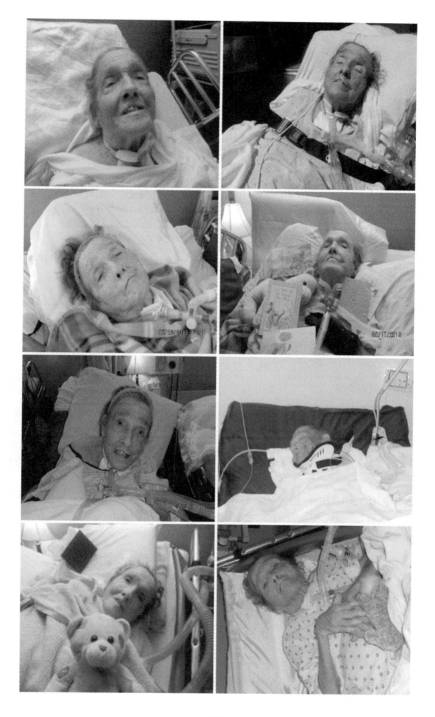

153

Mother's Unforgettable Words

"I just want to go home a little while."

In response to being told she had received the last rights three times. Mother laughed and said

"Oh, my goodness.
I want a cheeseburger and a cup of coffee."

During a time it took tremendous energy, work and persistence attempting to replace mother's wheelchair. A challenging time...

"I think I can do it. I want my life back. I don't mind working. I like work. I'll go back to work." ...

"Take me with you."

"Where are all my people?"

Talking about the book and the children she served at Shepard School...

"It's good they know. They understand... I taught them to be young ladies and gentlemen."

"I like to eat. I'm usually hungry."

"All my life I've had to fight for survival learn, learn, learn--to know what to do..."

"I've done anything that any able-bodied person could do. I've lived as complete a life as anybody could live."

. . .

Angela's Voice

Dear Mother,

Today is Monday, April 15th. (2013) We left Tahiti yesterday late afternoon. Bob and I were part of a tour taking a jeep up into the mountains. We stopped for lunch at a beautiful hotel. Bob slipped going into the bathroom, and I think knocked himself out. Fortunately he will be okay. He had to have stitches and we're told will have a pretty ugly black eye, but he should be fine. It was scary. It could have been far worse. The bathroom was down several flights of steps, and when entered there were no lights, and it was slippery. So, we are on our way back to Los Angeles. It will take 8 days to make it by ship.

I was up early today and thinking more about what would help you restore and get your life back. One thing that could be helpful is sunlight. You hardly get any there. I hope they open the window curtains for you each day. I hope you get up in a chair and get to move around a bit. I know this is not enough. What about getting one of the lights that replicate 'sunlight' and putting it near you. I can find one when I get back. Also, I don't know if you are reminded of the days and weeks and even hours of the day. Here, it is difficult to remember one from the next--not hard on shore days when we visit beautiful sights, but the daily sameness makes the days a challenge to remember.

I am told you are resting on full support and requiring the breathing machine. I'm told you are comfortable and being checked on regularly. I have some other ideas, mother. I know you were doing a fantastic job breathing on your own. I know after you left Barnes Hospital, the expectations and the resources for help were and are an issue at (name withheld). Your machine was placed on different settings, and the air being provided to you was arranged differently. I know in the past how you best used support, and this was different. I am glad you are safe, but I think you and I can resume a more involved way of getting you back to your life. You've always told me 'give you time' if you didn't seem all present. I think you are present, but too alone. For a 'people person' this isolation is much. Maybe the rest time is curative and you'll again make the most of it. I've had a lot of time to think about your accident and its consequences, and I think the most challenging is 'lack of expectation'. Unfortunately there are people who do not believe you can breathe unsupported. They believe you cannot get off the vent and that you can't make an independent life. I disagree. I know you, and you know you.

Mother said once she thought Bob (my amazing husband), might be spoiling her. She'd never been spoiled. I'm happy she had a time in her life when this was what she believed.

Bob would go and see mother with me during our many trips to Columbia (MO) and back again. He was with us when we went to Silver Dollar City in Branson and just about froze to death. If she mentioned anything she might like, need, or enjoy, he'd get it for her.

Mother was always ready to do anything! Even when she had serious wounds--she'd want to go. I couldn't find help and we started going to Candlewood Suites in Columbia and spending time working on the original book, cooking, doing. She'd bring the ingredients and tell me what she wanted and we'd get it done. We'd do her laundry and watch movies, or look at books and pictures. I was her hands and it let her see things she had saved forever.

I had no idea how grateful I would be for this simple and special time shared. I learned so much more than I knew, and I knew a lot. I just didn't know all she did to survive and thrive. Life was her greatest challenge and gift. Living and doing was her greatest accomplishment.

I could go on forever but I have to stop...

What Do I Know?

I know... mother did without meat so we children could have some protein; it weakened her bones, it hurt her health, but she sacrificed to take care of us.

I know... that when an organization or a family gave us a turkey for Thanksgiving, she had to cook the turkey, have most of the meat made into dressing and we'd have meat for many months to come.

I know... that she worked constantly, doing everything she could to bring in any amount of income so she could help daddy take care of us.

I know... that she did things that appeared impossible to be done, and she did them anyway. Then I saw her standing, sweating doing dishes, the chair underneath to catch her, until she almost needed to be able to rung out. You could see that much perspiration.

I know... that she did whatever it took to live. That her quest, her goal, her choice, her spirit wanted life so strongly, that there was nothing not worth the effort, the job to live.

I know... that she studied harder than anyone --learned more, she says than anyone could. She grew, she shared, she knew. I wanted to say, "and became the woman she is," but I no longer find those things to be truth. She returned to the woman, the person she was born and meant to be, and is now that light--that life--set free.

The things I remember, no--the things *I know* about mother and daddy's life are strong. Yet, the things I didn't know were only excavated or liberated during the time since I wrote the original '90-pound heavyweight' birthday book for mother, and more so since her horrible accident April 23, 2012.

Mother couldn't use her arms and hands to hug a child. At least not until much later in life when a difficult granddaughter required her to go beyond even her normal initiative (which was mighty) and find some way to let her know when she did something good. *Mother learned to hug!*

I missed that as a child. What she did do for me was to take a wet washrag and wipe my forehead. It felt like love. It was.

I also remember when it stopped. It was when she was pregnant with my youngest brother. I was around five. It was a loss.

I didn't know mother missed or regretted the inability to hug her children until I read a writing assignment from one of her occupational therapist school papers. Her task was to visit and interview disabled people and make a report. Mother again was amazing, and provided much learning for the student. As I'm writing this, I'm thinking I need to be more specific, but maybe not since there were many students who went on to many professional disciplines in life. Along her path she amazed them with her ability, attitude and determination to do just about anything. If she couldn't find a way she still made SOMETHING work.

Happy Mother's Day

May 11, 2014   *(after mother's death)*

Mother, wherever you are, and I personally think you went right up on the first escalator to God's Arms, I wish you Happy Mother's Day. I am sure many others join me with this remembering. You seem to be unforgettable, and I image for a woman who wanted to be known, this is about as good as it gets. You were known, and you are known! Your life is a guide, a light, and beacon for others. No, not everything was wonderful-- there were many hurts and fears, but I believe the final test rests in getting the job done--you did, and you did it with grace

I may not be on the fast track to sharing and letting more know about you but I am in the direction--I will get it done! It took a while for me to be able to remember, share, and be sure that my words were doing their intention to inspire and motivate, and not to blame and shame. You told me people aren't doing it wrong on purpose--they are doing the best they can. I accept part of this, and I believe we can all do a little better. That is my hope--that by learning and getting to know you, your life, your beliefs, and convictions, that others will pay a little more attention, and do a little more. We can do this!

The second tribute book CELEBRATE, the Life and Legacy of Janet Barnes, and her unsinkable, unstoppable, fighting spirit' is still in the works. It will be shared. The original '90-pound heavyweight, her story, words and life in vignette' has been shared and embraced by hundreds and even more who have read about you on the website, Facebook, and through my public sharing events. The revised edition is just about ready to print. It will share some of the amazing examples of living fully even after the horrific accident--in short, the miracles of everyday life!

When you went to God's Arms September 9, 2013, one month

before your 85th birthday, over a thousand people were saddened by the news and paid tribute to your life. You succeeded--you got off the ventilator not once but twice, you were present--talking, eating, telling jokes, and promoting mayonnaise as the ultimate condiment of choice. I hope I did it right. I hope you know you were a priority, a gift and blessing. I hope you remember me sharing with you the poem/song 'She's a Miracle, alright--God's Gift and God's Delight!

Love, Angela

Beyond Possible--Redefining Reality

May 29, 2012

Every day of her life she redefined reality. She and my dad did the impossible. They succeeded. Their lives, his and hers, raised the bar on what we individually and collectively think we can do, achieve, and be. The legacy of my mother, Janet Barnes, is her life--and it's me and you that know her, and choose to see more freely, more openly, and with more possibility because of her life, purpose and desire for you to know her.

Mother referenced a book *Mind Probe Hypnosis* by Irene Hicks. This was a philosophy I was exposed to in 2006 by another person, Edwene Gaines. I didn't pay much attention, and I am sure I discounted its value, merit and reality. Everything is/was challenged in me when I began the project of writing '90-pound heavyweight', Her Story, Words and Life in Vignette, and even more with the completion of the 'Life and Triumph of Janet Barnes', and the Celebration of her life.

The evolution of a heart and soul sometimes require a jump-start. Mine had been on a journey that I didn't recognize for quite a while. My soul unquestionably required CPR in 2009. The awareness and its impact is clear to me now, at 7:01 a.m.

As I sit here and think that mother may be dying now--this

160

moment--this timeframe. I am not with her. I am with her. Maybe I am more with her than I have ever been in my life. My heart, my peace, and my joy, I send to her--share with her. Her body, infiltrated with medication intended to battle the infection, is also taking life from her. She sleeps what appears to be a peaceful rest. Her battle, perhaps almost complete, is already won. I'm not counting her out, but she has won, and if peace, dignity, and angel's wings will tend her, and God's loving arms surround her, I release her.

I pray that she knows and accepts that she has done enough and is not seen in any way defective or unworthy. This has been a long-standing fear of hers all of her life. I declare it gone. I declare it removed from all cells and replace it with vibrant energy, maybe like the times she has escaped from reality and took a break from the 'too much'. This battle, this time she stayed present, and participated in her own destiny. She literally survived the impossible.

I announce to her, and to you, that mother 'got the job done-- with grace.' I don't know if she can physically, in what we call a literal sense, survive. I do know that she did survive. I do know that her life has made, and is making an indelible impact on what is called possible and real. She has done more with the significant physical limitations imposed on her than many, or most, able-bodied people. She now weighs less than ninety pounds, but remains a 90-pound heavyweight--a champ--a winner.

The gravest disease of society
--lack of expectation

and the contagious expression of negative, cancerous ideas, beliefs, expressions, words, and even actions. I'm out to do the best I can to eradicate this.

Angela Barnes 6/12/2013

Two Special Friends

One friend of mine, Marcia Miller, and one friend of Bob's, Don McAllister, were the people that came to see mother on a regular basis when she had to leave Missouri. They were there as support when I was absent so I wasn't so fearful of having her there alone. She needed people to be there to show her she wasn't alone.

Marcia Miller:

Her aura was so bright. I didn't know her. I knew you. I didn't know how we'd be together... I felt good seeing her and I felt good when I left--that karma thing.

We watched television. I'd read to her from magazines, helped her eat scrambled eggs and get a drink of water when she was permitted to have them. I'd put lotion on her and tidy up the room. When you took her away it was like my own mother was leaving.

Don McAlister

It was an honor and privilege to visit with Angela's mother, Janet Barnes, in the nursing home while Angela and Bob were away.

She was always pleasant and most times had a ready smile. She enjoyed me reading to her the many good wish cards, letters and notes. I also read to her the Reader's Digest magazine from front to back--many smiles there. At times I read to her while she was asleep. We also watched some TV if it was on when I was there.

What I was impressed with was her relationship with her nurses and staff. She knew what was going on, and she made the best of it.

She was strong mentally and physically, and made people around her believe this. I did. There should be more people like her.

She's a Miracle, Alright

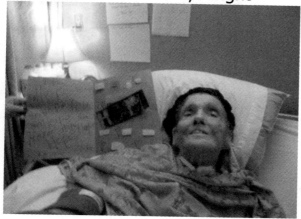

She's a miracle alright
God's gift and God's delight
A beacon shining bright
A guide to demonstrate
That life is right!

She's a miracle right here--right near
She's told her story well
Lived a life well spent
She's not done
She's more to share again

She's a miracle
A mighty heart within
She chooses life all over again
She knows the cost--expects to win
And lives life with a grin

She's battled fear
She's won the fight
She's stronger than an army of men
The 90-pound heavyweight
Shows us again

7/6/2012 (about 2 ½ months after the accident)

The Unfolding—United Prayer

these many months with fear so high
death literally so near
and yet the unstoppable spirit remained
life the greatest gift of all
in the heart of my mother
so as I tread on a trek
of fear, news, learning, hoping, praying
many of you have shared that journey with me
united prayers I believe aided her and her spirit
in the continued flow of life
the gift she prizes above all
so I stand here grateful that mother is not alone
and that united hearts join in prayer
and pave the way for her another day   8/27/2012

Redefined Reality

every day she redefined reality
did the impossible – succeeded
but life raised the bar on what we
individually and collectively
think we can do, achieve and be

the legacy is her life
fear has been a constant presence
yet determination has reigned supreme
as she faces more to do
I share my peace and joy with her

she has already won the battle
got the job done – with grace
she literally survived the impossible
so optimistically I see her
well, renewed and free

1/23/2013 (I am not yet as strong as mother)

What's A Prayer

it's a heart reaching
speaking
being touched--expanding
wanting the best
sharing that desire
connected

when you wonder
challenge or question
can I pray
do I believe
I think the answer is
yes

with each connected
concerned thought
desire for good
compassionate hearts
just know--do--share

and that's a prayer
it's not the name
it's the heart
and hearts
have the know-how
they do

4/29/2012

The Challenge

an opportunity
a chance to demonstrate
an alignment
reject confinement
a tangible way
to say okay
I'm here
I share--dare--care

it's going for it
reaching--stretching
exercising that right
to trust a little harder
do a little more
and go a little farther

4/29/2012

24 and 48 Hours

September 9 – 10, 2013 (after mother died)

It's been almost forty-eight hours. Time does give the mind a chance--it does not quiver, quake, and break.

I am not alone and I do know what to do. I am part of a legacy of strength, courage, know-how, gumption and initiative. It's not a gift I can reject. It's one with eyes wide open, I accept.

How many mistakes have I made? Each and every turn more mistakes were made. I can't play the "what did they not do" game here. I can't do it. It's not even fair to her. She chose life. She spent her last breath choosing life. She didn't quit.

I spent yesterday with mother, not knowing it was the last day of her life. We looked at magazines--saw a recipe for pumpkin soup we planned to make. We discussed the cost of gasoline, food, the news ... Her room had her pictures and personal items arranged. She had a hair appointment for the next day, and her long awaited wheelchair was to be delivered at 3:00 p.m. We looked at Facebook, the website, and I read her comments and posts (on my laptop.) She listened to audios from friends who left her messages. Mother called several people and talked to them. She told them she was coming back to see them and eventually coming home.

We talked about the independent apartment application that was submitted... I helped her eat her meal. She wasn't hungry and was having trouble breathing. I didn't know she was getting breathing treatments in her nose and not the trache where she breathed. She went to the ER that evening because she didn't feel well. They checked her out and found her in good shape, but dehydrated--good blood pressure and NOT SICK. The new facility...

I was to come back the next morning. I didn't yet know mother had spent her weekend getting known by several of the staff, sharing jokes, talking about grandchildren and more...

Did I do it right? I think so.

Allegory of the Long Spoons

The allegory of the long spoons is a parable that shows the difference between heaven and hell by means of people eating with long spoons. On the hell side they are starving and on the heaven side they are sated. The story can encourage people to be kind to each other. There are various interpretations of the fable including its use in sermons and in advice to lonely people.

The way I first heard the story was from mother describing a literal dinner at Jacob's Center in Columbia, Missouri, with a man who had one arm complaining about not being able to cut his meat and feed himself. I remember mother sounding irritated at him bemoaning his fate. She told me how he was fortunate to have an arm to use, and most of his body fully functioned.

I guess she was maybe mixing a story with the actual event, but my memory was that she and her contemporaries were seated at a feast. Many with missing limbs, mangled bodies. When they stopped complaining and feeling sorry for themselves they found a way to feed their neighbor--one with no arms was fed by one with an arm. One with no sight was served by a sighted person who in turn may have been helped by another who accommodated his challenge...

I found this interpretation on the internet, and I am paraphrasing it here:

I once visited an enchanted domain. I first visited hell and the sight was horrifying. Row after row of tables were laden with platters of sumptuous food, yet the people seated around the tables were pale, starving and moaning in hunger.

I came closer and I understood their predicament. Every person held a full spoon, but both arms were splinted with wooden slats so they could not bend either elbow to bring the food to their mouth. It broke my heart to hear the tortured groans of these people as they held their food so near but could not consume it.

Next I went to visit heaven. I was surprised to see the same thing I had witnessed in hell. Row after row of long tables laden with food, but in contrast to hell, the people here in heaven were sitting contentedly talking to each other--obviously full and nourished from their sumptuous meal.

As I came closer, I was amazed to discover here too, each person had his arm splinted on wood splints that prevented them from bending their elbows.

How did they manage to eat? I watched a man pick up his spoon and dig into the dish before him, then he stretched across the table and fed the person across from him. The recipient thanked him by leaning across the table to feed his benefactor.

I suddenly understood that heaven and hell offer the same circumstances and conditions. The critical difference is in the way the people treat each other.

I whispered in the ear of one starving man, you do not have to go hungry. Use your spoon to feed your neighbor and he will surely return the favor and feed you.

"You expect me to feed the despicable man sitting across the table?" said that man angrily. "I would rather starve than give him the pleasure of eating."

I then understood God's wisdom in choosing who is worthy to go to heaven, and who is to go to hell.

I personally do not agree with heaven or hell analogies, but I do see how we can make our own heaven on earth--or not.

What I am illustrating again is how my thoughts and beliefs align with mother's more than I knew. Thoughts align and agree-- and hopefully show you too, that 'attitude' and 'action' are ours to claim and proclaim. Whatever you choose to do can be done better together. I hope we do join and do better together!

Legacy Foundation

"Created and formed within twenty-four hours of mother's death, to make sense out of nonsense, and to share her unstoppable spirit!" Angela Barnes

90-pound heavyweight Janet Barnes Legacy Foundation a 501 (c) (3) Nonprofit organization.

Vision and Purpose of the Legacy Foundation:

To share how sheer determination, faith and a positive outlook can overcome any physical obstacles one may experience.

To encourage everyone to look past the "perceived" handicaps and "see" the potential within each person.

To serve as a catalyst for inclusion of the "human aspect" in medical training and practices. To foster, support and encourage the medical profession to care for the aged and physically challenged as aggressively as they care for the young (in accordance with the desires of the individual).

The Legacy Foundation is available to partner with medical schools, hospitals and organizations with books as well as a spokesperson to share the life and courage of a remarkable quadriplegic who lived a full and productive life for 84 years 11 months.

Through its website, at www.90poundheavyweight.org, individuals, as well as caregivers can be encouraged to look past appearances to see the potential of every human being.

The website will also encourage others to "tell their stories" thus sharing a wealth of knowledge through periodic blogs and progress reports.

To help identify where we have gaps that would benefit from knowing that life choice is a personal right and how we interact, respond, minimize and/or inhibit choice by lack of expectation is a serious condition at many of our institutions, and impacts how services and treatments are delivered or made available.

How can you can learn more and be part of the movement?

Dear reader, you can be a part and you are needed.

Through sharing Janet Barnes' story

Through volunteering at schools, hospitals, etc.

Posting comments and blogs to encourage others by sharing your insights and breakthroughs

Through supporting homeless individuals with meals, toiletries, blankets, clothing, etc.

By honoring and respecting all persons regardless of their physical or mental capacities

By helping to find volunteers, interns, other organizations to partner with the Legacy Foundation, in a variety of areas, i.e., public and media relations, research, website and technical support.

By recommending a book club and sponsoring a book pack or library deposit.

Through financial support of the Legacy Foundation with donations.

You may make tax deductible donations: on the website www.90poundheavyweight.org and click donations. You may also go to any Region's Bank and give the title 90-pound heavyweight Janet Barnes Legacy Foundation or PayPal legacy@90poundheavyweight.org

Post Script

February 19, 2015

This challenge required time. I had to grow tall enough to share a story that needed telling--or so I thought. I thought I had to tell you everything! I thought mother deserved it. I thought you needed, wanted or just had to know all that happened...

In the end you are getting the story of her life and a glimpse into her world after the accident. You are not getting 'it all'. I had to learn to step aside and let mother's life tell the story. She was strong (surname Strong).

I will have to let 'the more' wait for you to choose to know it. Maybe you will visit www.90poundheavyweight.org, the legacy foundation established to share, promote education and remember mother in ways that touch and change people. Perhaps you will be part of the movement to challenge our medical ideas, ideals, practices and world. I hope to be able to share more glimpses of her amazing life with a virtual library. I hope to attract interns, volunteers and people to be part of the 'possible'. The stretch is worth it.

Regardless, I am changed. I am better, and I know that I did not fail her. I did it right. I know she knew whatever was needed--desired--was available and that her independence and life was the priority. So, now you know it too.

Yes, dear mother, you did more than enough and
absolutely deserved the air you breathed.

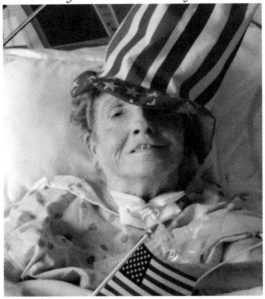

You're not supposed to be proud of yourself, but I was proud of my life.
I lived a life well lived. My muscles were terrible. I couldn't lift anything,
but my mind compensated for my lack of muscle. Janet Barnes
October 9, 1928 ~~ September 9, 2013

About the Author

With sincerity and vulnerability Angela Barnes writes of her mother from her heart. Her poetry and songs are a mixture of hurts and fears – often raw and sometimes caustic – to a transcendence of hopefulness through uplifting and awe-inspiring language.

She shares her life's journey of growing up in a household where both parents were "differently able" (quadriplegic and paraplegic). She shares how poetry served as an avenue through which she could visit her pain, frustrations, shame, anger and guilt. She found that poetry gave her an internal voice which later led to an emerging willingness to reveal a voice of authenticity.

In writing about her mother's extraordinary life of fierce determination and will to live life fully, regardless of appearances Angela found in herself a deep compassion not only for her mother (*a 90-pound heavyweight*), but for all others who were in pain because of their particular circumstances. She began experiencing life both as an observer and as a participant.

After over five decades of expressing her feelings through poetry and later documenting her mother's exceptional life, she realized the awesome power of her voice. She began to understand the healing power of speaking the truth boldly, even when it was soul-paining. She further realized that each event she encountered shaped her life – resulting in the emergence of a new and dynamic voice – one that is empowered and empowering.

Her constant question "Who Am I" was answered through her writings:

A devoted daughter to remarkable parents

A mother of two daughters whom she loves dearly

A wife of a most amazing man

A creative individual

A writer

A partial listing of her writings follow:

The FACES OF MOTHER A limited edition photo journey sharing the life of Janet Barnes, featuring unique and unpublished pictures that capture her life in expression.

ONE FOOT IN FRONT OF THE OTHER An un-literary anthology of Poetry, Words and Thoughts--also available in excerpts spans five decades of writing.

BAMBOOZLED and Outmaneuvered…he says…she says.. Uncensored. A light hearted romance and true story by my husband Robert Haug and I. Bob calls it his freedom of speech book.

Mini-books are photo journeys/collections that included 'GLIMPSES' AND 'TOUCHES' of a variety of topics and venues. Books can be commissioned for almost any topic.

The first 'Glimpse of India', aka finding loving in the mist and growing brave enough to fall in love.

Touch of Beauty FLOWERS--a beauty deficit remedy.

Touch of Beauty ICE CRYSTAL DELIGHT--captured the ice storm illustrating and contrasting beauty in all its form.

FEED ME…FEED ME…PLEASE FEED ME. A collection of original recipes, poems, songs and things I know that I know to feed the body, heart and soul.

LOVE, ACCEPTANCE AND NO BITCH'N Documents how a year of acceptance and love can make for a brand new me from the inside-out.

> *Angela is a motivational speaker, author, poetry concert consultant and continues to share her heart spoken words through a variety of channels both online and in person.*

Dear Reader:

Thank you for your interest in mother's triumphs, and for supporting the Legacy Foundation. I would very much like to hear from you.

What takeaways or in what way has mother's story and life made a difference to you?

Please share mother in whatever way works for you.

Your thoughts are welcome to be shared in the series titled: "Grandma Janet: aka Lessons learned from '90-pound heavyweight, Janet Barnes'"

Respond to one of the following:

www.heartspokenwords.com

www.90poundheavyweight.org

legacyfoundation@90poundheavyweight.org

Legacy Foundation 331 Chamberlin Ave. Fairview Heights IL 62208

First Responders, Schools, Medical Programs and other groups are welcome to contact us and learn how "anyone who needs or wants the book" will get a book program. Our goal is to share. Together we can do it.

Join the Legacy program and hear special subscriber's audio recordings of mother.

Be informed of new releases, trivia contests and more.

Receive e-book offerings.

Charter fan clubs and book clubs receive surprises and bonuses.

Angela